Between the Realms
Cornish Myth and Magic

BETWEEN
the
REALMS
Cornish Myth and Magic

by
Cheryl Straffon

Line illustrations by Gemma Gary

TROY BOOKS

First Edition
Printed October 2013

ISBN 978-1-909602-06-9

Published by Troy Books
www.troybooks.co.uk

Troy Books Publishing
BM Box 8003
London WC1N 3XX

Other publications by Cheryl Straffon

EM Guide to Ancient Sites in West Penwith [Meyn Mamvro publications, 1992, 2010]
EM Guides to Bodmin Moor & North Cornwall, Mid-Cornwall & the Lizard, and Isles of Scilly [Meyn Mamvro publications, 1993-5]
Pagan Cornwall: land of the Goddess [Meyn Mamvro publications, 1993, 2012]
The Earth Goddess [Blandford, 1997]
Fentynyow Kernow: in search of Cornwall's holy wells [Meyn Mamvro publications, 1998, 2005]
Megalithic Mysteries of Cornwall [Meyn Mamvro publications, 2004]
Daughters of the Earth [O Books, 2007]
With Lana Jarvis: The Goddess in Crete: a guide to Minoan sites [Dor Dama press, 2014]

Also: Editor of Meyn Mamvro magazine [www.meynmamvro.co.uk] & Goddess Alive! Magazine [www.goddessalive.co.uk]

Contents

Photographs between pages 96 - 97
Photographs by author
3. Boleigh Fogou - West Penwith, Cornwall
4. Balowall Barrow - West Penwith, Cornwall
8. The Blind Fiddler - West Penwith, Cornwall
9. Trencrom Hill - Near Hayle, Cornwall

Photographs by Jane Cox
1. Boscawen Un Stone Circle - West Penwith, Cornwall
2. The Merry Maidens - West Penwith, Cornwall
5. Duloe Circle - Nr Looe, Cornwall
6. Carn Euny Fougo - West Penwith, Cornwall
7. Mermaid of Zennor, Bench-end - Zennor Church, Cornwall
10. The Logan Stone - Zennor, Cornwall
11. Mên Scryfa, standing stone - West Penwith, Cornwall

Introduction

Cornwall has a rich collection of traditional tales, stories, myths, legends and folklore. Very often they tell of encounters with supernatural beings, such as fairies, piskeys, mermaids, witches, giants and other strange creatures. Many of these stories were probably transmitted orally for hundreds if not thousands of years before they were written down. Too often they are presented nowadays as quaint survivals of a long-lost era, one that was governed by superstition and irrationality. However, I have always believed that there is a lot more in these stories and legends than meets the eye. Although some stories were undoubtedly embellished, and in some cases created, in the Victorian era, nevertheless a significant number of them seem to have a ring of authenticity about them, and often, unbeknown to those who tell the stories or transmit them onto the printed page, seem to speak of the same kinds of themes and narratives that we find in much earlier works. These include the Irish sagas and the Welsh mythic tales that date from the early medieval period, but refer to beliefs and events that were current many centuries before. In addition, if we turn to the beliefs and practices of many native indigenous peoples from around the world, we find that, despite individual differences, many of them share the same way of interfacing with the world of magic and spirit, traces of which we can also find in the Cornish material.

These themes and these materials are many and various, but what unites them all is what I have called in the title of this book – 'Between the Realms'. A 'realm' is a sphere or domain, and for most of the time we occupy one domain: the here and now, the mundane world, the place and time that we fill in our everyday lives. But this is not the only realm, as has been recognised ever since humankind developed as a species. In all cultures and in all societies, people have been aware of other realms outside the everyday world. Different religions have given these realms different names, which we can perhaps summarise as the world of spirit, or the Otherworld. This world can be accessed by a variety of techniques that can lead to a state of altered consciousness, and sometimes the Otherworld comes unbidden into our world. On special occasions we can enter this Otherworld, which is generally populated by otherworldly beings, and also by the spirits of the dead from our own world. It is the world of the ancestors, of strange zoomorphic animals and beings, of 'little people' and giants, and of the gods and goddesses of old (who become the devil and all his cohorts under Christianity). It is a realm that has some similarities to our own, but one that is also strangely unfamiliar. It is a dangerous world to enter, but nevertheless one that can give new insights and experiences that change our world view when we return to our mundane world.

This book then is about this Otherworld, and how it manifests in our world. It is about how we can sometimes step from our world into that Otherworld, and how sometimes that Otherworld appears in our world. It is about how our ancestors, the megalithic people who have left their monuments for us to marvel about, viewed that world and connected with it; and about how people in Cornwall ever since have had experiences of that world and recorded those experiences in the stories, myths and legends that they transmitted orally for a long time before finally being written down .In the following 15 chapters, I will examine different aspects and perspectives of the experience of being 'between the realms' through source material from Cornish myth and magic. I have drawn on some of my previous writings (particularly in chapters 1 to 8) in 'Meyn Mamvro' magazine that I have produced and edited for the last 28 years, though I have updated and added to many of those articles. And I have also drawn on the ideas and writings of others in this field, which I have also acknowledged throughout. But this is, to the best of my knowledge, the first time this material has all been brought together in one place and given a coherent structure in this way.

My thanks go to all those who have given me ideas and material for this book, and my special thanks go to Lana Jarvis, who has so often walked between the realms with me, and edited and proof read the manuscript. My thanks also to Gemma Gary for the fine illustrations that accompany the text. Finally, the book is dedicated to Solly, who gave me such insights of wonder and magic when he was alive, and now himself walks his path in the Otherworld.

Cheryl Straffon
May 2013

Chapter One

Rituals and Rites at Cornish Sites

It is now generally recognised that megalithic sites were built primarily for ritual and religious purposes, even if we do not know the precise nature of those rituals. Although the Neolithic and Bronze Age peoples left no written records, a number of clues can be found in both the construction of the sites, and the legends that have become attached to them.

For centuries, a legend has persisted that at the Cheesewring on Bodmin Moor, a druid-priest possessed a magnificent golden cup. Whenever a huntsman came by, the druid would offer him a drink from the cup, which was inexhaustible. One day a hunter who was determined to drink the cup dry took the cup from the druid and drank the wine until he could drink no more. Unable to empty the cup, he angrily made off with it, only to plunge to his death off the rocks, where he and the cup were buried under a round cairn of stones. As well as having echoes of the bottomless cauldron of Cerridwen (from the Welsh *Mabinogian* text), the legend also hints at memories of a druidic priesthood, who provided, through their knowledge of when to plant and reap, the means of sustenance for the tribe, and the perils of challenging or interfering with their wisdom. A twist to the tale is that in 1818 the Rillaton cairn was excavated, not far from the Cheesewring, and the skeleton of a man, a bronze dagger, and a gold cup were found! Although the legend was not written down until after this date, it is likely that it was in the oral tradition before this, and indeed could have been passed down the generations since the burial itself.

The Rillaton barrow itself is near the Hurlers stone circle, reputedly men turned to stone for playing at hurling on a Sunday, a legend almost identical to that of many other stone circles in Cornwall, including the Merry Maidens, Tregeseal and Boscawen-ûn stone circles in West Penwith, the Nine Maidens stone circle at Wendron, and the Nine Maidens stone row on St.Breock Downs. This may well be a folk memory of the use of the sites in pre-Christian times by groups of priests or priestesses for ritual and ceremony, that included dancing and movement. There is some archaeological evidence that dancing was performed at stone circles in the late Neolithic and early Bronze Ages, and together with drumming, chanting and the ingestion of narcotic herbs and plants, would all have been tools to allow the shamans and shamankas to enter trance states in order to commune with the guardian spirits of the sites and the dead ancestors.

Other sites have legends too that tell of former ritualistic practices. At Rosmerryn, a few hundred metres from the Merry Maidens stone circle, lies a fogou, an underground chamber dating from the Iron Age, a much later period than the stone circle. But it too has a legend: this time of the devil who was seen piping to the witches who formerly held their sabbats there, a most direct memory of pagan rites held there. This legend is very close to that of the Merry Maidens: in both a figure who is a Piper plays wild and strange music for a group of women (maidens at the stone circle, witches in the fogou) who dance around. They are both surely the same memory of the same pagan ritual performed in the area, either at the time of the building of the sites or later.

At the Mên-an-Tol in West Penwith the legend that if you want to be cured of ailments you must crawl through the holed stone nine times widdershins (against the sun), is perhaps a memory of this circular dance, itself a reflection of the movement of the sun and moon throughout the skies.

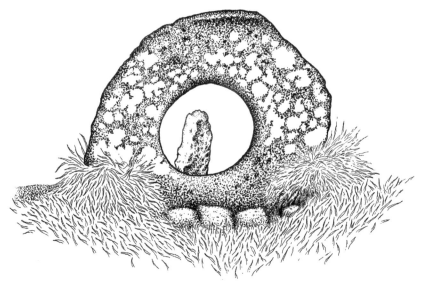

Nine as a number keeps recurring: nine times widdershins, the 'Nine Maidens' stone circle, etc. Nine may have become a sacred number because it represented the months of a pregnancy, which itself may have been seen as intrinsically related to the lunar cycles.

More dancing was seen at Balowall Barrow (Carn Glûze), a large round barrow near to St.Just, but this time the legend is of lights burning and rings of fairies dancing in and around it on moonlit nights. Fairies are another name for the ancient tomb builders, either themselves or their spirits, and it has been observed that "this is a folk memory perhaps of sacred rituals that were once performed by the last of the megalith builders".[1]

Burial chambers are one kind of site where rituals obviously took place. Aubrey Burl has remarked: "Gradually through the generations, the great megalithic mounds became temples as well as tombs, shrines where rituals were performed to honour the dead and ask for their assistance".[2] Many of the entrances of the chambered tombs are oriented so as to bring the dead into association with the moon or sun, for example midwinter solstice sunrise at Newgrange in Ireland, Gavrinis in Brittany, and Bosiliack Barrow in West Penwith; and midwinter solstice sunset at Maes Howe on Orkney, and Balowall Barrow in West Penwith. From Chûn Quoit there is a perfect midwinter solstice sunset over

---

1. 'Belerion' – Craig Weatherhill [Alison Hodge, 1981]
2. 'Rites of the Gods' – Aubrey Burl [Dent, 1981]

Carn Kenidjack, where the sun sets into a notch in the rocky outcrop. Also, all of West Penwith's entrance graves (with one exception) are oriented between SE (midwinter solstice sunrise) and SW (midwinter solstice sunset), and fogous too, although from a later period, have the orientation of their longest passage to the midsummer solstice sunrise or sunset.

In addition, some sites have curious entrance holes, which may have been made to allow the spirits of the dead to emerge for communion with the living, or to allow them safe passage to the other world. One such example is the cutaway in the dividing slab of Trethevey Quoit near Bodmin Moor. The cupmarks on the top of Chûn Quoit and Mulfra Quoit may also have had ritual significance, perhaps as places where libations to the dead were left, a practice still carried out until fairly recent times in Brittany. This has parallels with the burial found under Try menhir in West Penwith, which consisted of a cist which had contained a cremation with a beaker and an offering of meat. In other places the dead were buried in a ritualistic or symbolic way, perhaps facing a certain direction. Usually bodies were placed facing east or west for the rising or setting sun, but when the Bronze Age burial cemetery was excavated at Harlyn Bay near Padstow, it was found that all the bodies had been placed with their heads facing magnetic north. Clearly here there was a ritual practice that showed an intrinsic knowledge of the magnetic properties of the earth, something that experienced dowsers can find today without the aid of a compass.

To many of these tombs of the dead were brought sacred offerings to make them monuments for the living. Time and again these offerings consisted of quartz. The sacredness of white quartz is well attested: large quartz stones were used to line the entrance of Newgrange in Ireland for the midwinter sun; to denote the Samhain sunset at Boscawen-ûn stone circle in West Penwith; to construct the whole stone circle at Duloe in SE Cornwall; and to mark the orientation of Pendeen fogou in West Penwith, where the passage takes a sharp left-hand bend. At many more sites in Britain, excavation has found small white quartz pieces brought to the site as an offering during the construction. In Cornwall this happened at the Harlyn Bay cemetery; at the Hurlers stone circle on Bodmin Moor, where there was a floor of crushed quartz underlying the central circle; under a barrow at St.Eval, surrounding the Mên Gurtha stone on St.Breock Downs: in the pit of a menhir on Longstone Downs near St.Austell; and at a ritual site on Trethellan Farm near Newquay.

Aubrey Burl speculates that these quartz stones may have been viewed as soul-stones, symbolising the moon to where the spirits of the dead had gone: "Quartz was believed to have protective powers, and increasingly in the Bronze Age in many parts of the British Isles, pieces of it were placed with the dead".[3]

In other places other kinds of offerings were left. At Gûn Rith standing stone, near the Merry Maidens in West Penwith, a beach pebble was found, perhaps indicating that some ritual involving invocation of a sea goddess had taken place there. A similar pebble was found in Obadiah's Barrow on Gugh on the Isles of Scilly, and on the Cornish mainland at Carn Creis barrow, lying between St.Just and Sennen, a rich array of grave goods were found, including twelve bright blue faience beads, the base of a leaf-shaped arrowhead, and a perforated heart-shaped stone. At Escalls Carn barrow on the cliff at Sennen, a burial cist contained flints and shells, once again emphasising a connection to the sea.

---

3. 'Rites of the Gods' – Aubrey Burl [Dent, 1981]

Other grave goods, such as pottery, urns, glass beads, hammer stones and bronze fragments (perhaps from pendant ornaments or ear-rings) have been found in Scillonian entrance graves. On the mainland of Cornwall, it seems that axes had ritual significance for the dead. In a number of barrows, (for example Botrea Hill near St.Just) axe heads have been found, suggesting a ritual significance. The prehistoric Cornish axe industry was a thriving concern, and Cornish axes have been found in many burial sites all over Britain. The axe heads carved on the centre stone of Boscawen-ûn circle, visible only at the midsummer solstice sunrise, may be an indication of the local importance of the cult.

All of this points to an ancestor cult of the dead, and the possible ritual activity associated with it. This may have included the deposition of animal skulls and bones, grave goods (including beads, arrowheads, pebbles and jewellery), offerings of wine or milk or honey; quartz stones, and soils representing fertility or rebirth. At the tombs of the dead there would have been feasting and merrymaking and ceremonial activities that involved dancing, drumming, piping, chanting and spirit journeying. The dead were thought to have gone to an afterlife, but their spirits remained with the tribe and continued to be present in the tombs and megalithic monuments built to honour them. Ritual was not just a part of their lives: it was the way they lived their lives, and an understanding of this unlocks the key into the world of our megalithic ancestors.

Chapter Two

Shamans and Druids

When trying to understand the past, we have to put forward a hypothesis from possible interpretations. The earliest periods (Neolithic, Bronze Age & early Iron Age) have left no written records, and from the later Iron Age, or so-called Celtic period, we only have records that were written down much later, usually by Christian monks. So it is to the fields of archaeology and comparative anthropology that we must turn for evidence to try and understand the past. Archaeology can tell us much about the sites and their development from pottery, artefacts and burial remains, but when we turn to the spiritual beliefs of our prehistoric ancestors it is on much more shaky ground. Nevertheless, it is possible to put together a suggested scenario of how the spiritual leaders of the people may have mediated with the world of spirit and deity, based on archaeological finds, by the writings of early historians, and by comparative anthropology, that is, by comparing the native tribes of Britain, and in particular Cornwall, with the practices of other native tribes that we know about in the 19th & 20th centuries from around the world, who were living a stone age lifestyle. From all of this, we may be able to gain an insight into the Shamans and Druids of Cornish prehistory.

So who were the Shamans? We know that in most tribes living a stone age lifestyle (such as native peoples in New Guinea, Indonesia and South America) that certain people are singled out by the tribe to take on the role of contacting the spirit world. This can vary a great deal from tribe to tribe: sometimes it is one person who performs that function, sometimes several, sometimes most of the tribe take part in such ceremonies. These people have generally come to be known as Shamans, which can be people of either sex, though sometimes the word Shamanka is used for female shamans. Strictly speaking, the word should only be used when talking about the Ural-Altaic people of Siberia, from where the word is derived, but it has by extension come to be applied to similar kinds of spiritual mediators from most native tribes. In the 19th and early 20th centuries, writers sometimes used to refer to them as 'witch doctors' or 'medicine men' but the term shaman now seems to have become prevalent. We know that there are shamans in most of the tribes living stone age lifestyles today (now sadly diminishing rapidly as the inexorable rise of 20th & 21st century 'civilisation' takes over the lifestyle of the world's last remaining indigenous peoples). So it is reasonable to assume that the Neolithic (New Stone Age) people of Britain must have had similar spiritual leaders. Some time after Britain separated from the Continent in about 8000 BCE, the foraging people (also called the Hunter-Gatherers) from the Mesolithic (Middle Stone Age) era began to settle in more permanent camps and dwellings. From this settling (which probably happened over several centuries if not millennia) came the first permanent houses and hut circles, which marked the emergence of the Neolithic era c.3500 BCE.

The people then began to build their first megalithic structures, the dolmens or cromlechs, remains of which can still be found in Ireland, Wales and Cornwall. In Cornwall, good examples can be found in West Penwith at Chûn, Mulfra, Lanyon (now rebuilt) and Zennor, and on the edge of Bodmin Moor at Trethevey. These dolmens, sometimes called Quoits in Cornwall, consisted of a box-like structure enclosed in a mound of earth, with a capstone at the top, probably deliberately exposed. This flat capstone may have been used for the purpose of excarnation, the practice known about from elsewhere, whereby dead bodies are left on a high platform for the carrion birds and animals to pick off the flesh. The bones may then have been placed into the dolmens inside the mound, Although few bones have been found in Cornwall because of the acidic soils, we know from elsewhere that these bones were disarticulated - that is, bits of bones from different individuals would be placed together, and later some bones would be removed and replaced by others. The implication of this is that the burials were thought of as communal, and the buried people all as interrelated members of the same family group. The archaeologist Paul Bonnington has described it as the burial of people being "absorbed into the ancestral body".[4]

What was the purpose then of these communal burials? We may imagine that at specific times, the Shamans from the tribe would ascend the hills to enter the mounds of these dolmens and there attain some altered state of consciousness, by means perhaps of fasting, rhythmic repetition, or the ingestion of narcotic substances. Most indigenous peoples use local psychotropic substances to attain states of altered consciousness, such as the Mexican peyote or the South American ayahuasca plants. In Cornwall,

---

4. *Pers. Com.*

many of the dolmens lie on high moorland, and even to this day magic mushrooms can be found growing naturally in the vicinity. If these grew here 5000 years ago (and perhaps other plants that have now disappeared) then the shamans would readily use these substances to help them on their spirit journeys to meet the spirits of their ancestors buried within the dolmens. We know from other peoples that these spirit journeys are often undertaken to learn the secrets of healing and understanding the patterns and meaning of the universe, so the shamans of Neolithic Cornwall may have been doing something very similar.

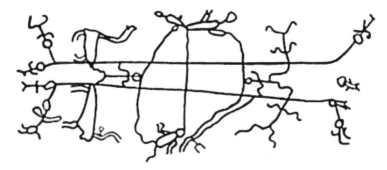

Chukchi drawing of mushroom spirits
[collected by W.Borgoras, 1905]

This practice probably went on for many centuries, but when we reach the early Bronze Age different kinds of structures were being built, particularly barrows. These barrows may have been used in similar ways to the dolmens, though it is interesting to note that of the excavated barrows in Cornwall, only 55% contained burial remains and 41% contained no remains at all. Of the ones that contained remains, only 4% were deposited there from an earlier structure. So it does appear that the fashion of adding bones into the chambers, that was practised in the Neolithic period, had changed by the Bronze Age. Of course, the barrows may have continued to be places for the shamans of the tribe to go on spirit journeys: over a half of the barrows *did* have deposits of bones, and even in those that did not, the function of the barrow may have been similar. They may have been built as a monument to the Ancestors, manifesting the presence of the dead in the land of the living, without the necessity of placing actual bones inside.

If we move forward from the Bronze Age to the Iron Age, and particularly the Romano-Celtic period of about 500 BCE - 500 CE, we can see a definite change in the structures where people lived. In Cornwall, people were living in Courtyard House settlements and constructing large earth works in the form of so-called 'hill forts', cliff castles and rounds. They were also making fine bronze, copper and gold ornaments. It used to be thought that this was all a result of the movement into Cornwall by 'Celtic' peoples from the Continent, bringing with them the culture known generally as La Tène and Halstatt, named after the places in Switzerland and Austria where the distinctive 'Celtic' styles were first found. However, it has been shown recently by genetic research that the 'Celtic' people of Cornwall were in fact descendants of their Neolithic and Bronze Age forebears, and therefore inhabited the same land and were surrounded by the sacred monuments left by *their* ancestors. They may have adopted some of the cultural styles of their continental cousins, but there was no great invasion of peoples into Cornwall.

Our knowledge of these so-called 'Celtic' peoples who lived in Britain prior to the Roman invasion in 43 CE comes mainly from Roman writers, in particular Tacitus. He tells of a priestly caste of Druids who ministered to the spiritual needs of the Celtic tribes, and according to him, these Druids were finally attacked and defeated on the Isle of Anglesey by Suetonius Paulinus in about 60 CE, and their sacred groves destroyed. This account implies that the Druids had by then abandoned the megalithic monuments of their predecessors, and instead worshipped in woodland groves. There may be some truth in all of this - but is it necessarily the whole story? The Celtic tribe occupying Cornwall at this time was the Cornovii, but we have little evidence of specific sacred groves, except for the clue left by the Celtic name *neved* or *neves*, which means 'a sacred grove'. There are a number of Cornish place names derived from this word, such as Carnevas (near St.Merryn), Lanivet (near Bodmin), Trenovissick (near St.Blazey) and Trewarnevas (near St.Anthony-in-Meneage).

However, what we do have in Cornwall, and only in Cornwall, from this period are the fogous. Fogous were constructed always in association with Courtyard House settlements, and we know from the excavations at Carn Euny that the fogou was there before the Courtyard House settlement that grew up around it. If this were the case at other settlements as well, it implies that these structures were built right at the beginning of the Romano-Celtic period (prior to 500 BCE) and were important enough to be maintained and used for about 1000 years, the period of the 'Celts' and their priestly caste the Druids.

The function of fogous has been much disputed in the past, but the general consensus nowadays by nearly everyone, including archaeologists, is that they were used for ritual and ceremonial purposes. Both ends of the fogou were sealed, and entry was effected by the narrow creep passage. This meant that whoever entered the underground chamber had to do so on their belly or hands and knees, so that entering the dark cavern must have been a powerful experience. This begins to sound like the entering of the dolmens by the Neolithic shamans! Could we have here in

Cornwall a continuity of purpose by the religious leaders of the community from the Neolithic to the Romano-Celtic period? In the Neolithic the shamans entered the earth mounds of the dolmens to commune with the spirits of the dead and the ancestors; in the Bronze Age their successors went to the barrows for the same purpose; and finally in the Iron Age/Celtic period the Druids, spiritual successors of the shamans, went to the fogous for the self-same purpose.

We can perhaps imagine the Druids spiritual mediators preparing themselves by achieving an altered state of consciousness and then entering the fogou by the creep passage into the darkness to go on a spirit journey to meet the spirits of the dead ancestors. They would then return to the tribe with that knowledge, perhaps released from the darkness at the moment of the summer solstice sunrise or sunset (all fogous are oriented in those directions). Of course this can only be speculation, but if it is true, then the Druids were the natural successors of the shamans and inherited their wisdom and practised it in new but similar settings. This would be an amazing continuity of spiritual tradition stretching over thousands of years from prehistoric Shaman to Celtic Druid.

Chapter Three

The Fairy Lands

Many of the legends and stories of Fairy Folk that are common to all Celtic countries (Ireland, Cornwall, Wales, Isle of Man, Scotland & Brittany) contain elements that hint at the ancient significance of the 'genus loci' or "spirit of place". To our early ancestors, many of the places of the land were infused with the spirit of that land, and what to us may appear to be inanimate objects, such as stones, rocks and trees, were the embodiment and living place of the spirits of the earth, in ancient times the Goddess herself. For example, In Ireland and Scotland the little people were known to inhabit certain places, usually ancient hilltops, 'fairy knolls', and prehistoric earthworks. This is reflected in the names of some Irish places, such as "mullach na sidhe"[5] the fairy mound, or "slieve gullion" = the enchanted mountain. In the recent re-mapping of Ireland by the Irish O.S some 30,000 such sites have been identified! In the Isle of Man there were many fairy glens - indeed there was hardly a glen or hollow that was not their

---

5. Sidhe (pronounced 'shee') in Irish Gaelic, Sithe in Scottish Gaelic, and Shee in Manx are etymologically identical.

haunt. Their memory remains in some of the place-names: "cronk ny shee" the hill of the fairy, and "glion ny shee" the glen of the fairy. "Glenshee" in Scotland is the same word. Wales too has its fairy glens, at Betws-y-Coed and Penmaenmawr, which lies near the Bronze Age 'Druids Circle'. The dolmen at Pentre Ifan was also known to be the haunt of fairies, as was the mound of Corriecatachan on Skye where the fairies danced on moonlit nights.

In Cornwall, the name pisky has been applied to both natural features, such as Piskey's Cove near Mount's Bay, and Piskie Fields in Madron and Lelant, and also megalithic structures, such as Piskey Hall fogou at Constantine. The piskeys and spriggans ("spyrysyon" in Cornish) were thought to inhabit the old ruins and megaliths as well as the high places, and this could perhaps be a folk memory of the small-statured Neolithic people who built them. Very often the places of Fairy are the sacred places of the ancestors. Caroy Church on Skye is built on the site of a prehistoric burial mound, but below that it was thought to be fairy ground, and their songs could be heard rising through the earth. In Ireland there were two such places: one was at Tara, the magical and sacred centre of the island. As Evans-Wenz noted: "On the ancient hill of Tara, from whose heights the High Kings once ruled all Ireland, from where the sacred fires in pagan days announced the annual resurrection of the sun, the Easter Tide, where the magic of Patrick prevailed over the magic of the Druids, and where the hosts of the Tuatha De Danann were wont to appear at the great Feast of Samhain, today the fairy-folk of modern times hold undisputed sovereignty." [6] The other place was Lough Gur (in Co. Limerick). Wenz described it as "a very sacred spot, a mystic centre for pilgrimages and for the

---

6. 'The Fairy Faith in Celtic Countries' – W.Y.Evans Wentz [OUP, 1911]

celebration of Celtic religious rites." [7] On the two hills near Lough Gur, sacred rites to the ancient Goddesses Aine and Fennel (Finren) were celebrated, a hint that the fairy places may originally have been places of the Goddess.

The most fairy-haunted part of the Isle of Man was the southern slopes of South Barrule, the mountain on whose summit the ancient god of Man, Mananin in was said to have had his stronghold. In Wales the cromlech of Pentre Ifan, already mentioned, was also known as the 'Womb or Court of Cerridwen', the ancient Celtic Goddess. In Cornwall the fairies often occupied places ruled over by the giants, for example Trencrom Hill, where the spriggans guarded the buried treasure, was controlled by the giant Trecrobben, which may be a possible memory of a former god worshipped there, just as the giant-killer Jack the Tinker may be a late corruption of the Celtic god Lugh. The fishermen at Newlyn also used to leave part of their catch out for the Buccas,[8] a propitiation to a possible former sea-god/goddess. The same custom existed on Lewis in Scotland where libations were poured to the Shoney in order to bring in the seaweed.

Many fairy places were entrances to otherworlds, places where the veil between this world and the other world was at its thinnest; for example Lough Gur in Ireland was known as the entrance of Tir-na-Nog, the Celtic otherworld of eternal youth. One such place in Cornwall was The Gump near St Just where piskey folk and visions of otherworldly spirits were seen, and the whole area has legends of the spirits of the dead associated with it. At Mousehole, also in West Penwith, troops of small people used to come out of a hole in the cliff opening onto the beach, perhaps a memory

---

7. 'The Fairy Faith in Celtic Countries' – W.Y.Evans Wentz [OUP, 1911]

8. Cornish Bucca is equivalent to the Irish 'pooka' and the Welsh 'pwca'.

of the occupancy of caves by ancient peoples. There is a similar legend on Skye where the Pipers Cave was thought to connect with Fairyland. In Wales it was lakes and places along the sea-coast of Pembrokeshire that provided the contact with the little people, and Man too has the same tradition - one of the last places the little people[9] were seen was at Lough Goayr in Kirkbride one summer evening at dusk, shouting "Hoi son n'herln!" (Hey for Ireland!).

The area of fairyland, though extensive, was often quite boundried. Water provided one boundary. In Ireland if pursued by fairies escape might be effected by crossing a stream. In Man the moving water in the Glens were the places were the fairies loved to sing and dance. Also in Man a boundary is marked in one story when a girl enters the fairy world by crawling through a gorsebush. In Cornwall Grace Hutchens (in the story of the fairy dwelling on Selena Moor) enters fairyland by wading a brook and entering an orchard where she hears music at a distance. Boundaries and pathways are actually very important to an understanding of fairylore, and provide a clue to the relationship of fairy to the sacred lines on the land. Some of the most interesting fairylore is to do with this. At Tara in Ireland fairies from Rath Ringlestown would form in a procession across Tara road and between two houses. One man went out of his house at the time of the procession and was later found dead, the fairies having taken him for interfering with their procession. Evans Wenz comments that fairy paths or fairy passes may be actual magnetic arteries through which circulates the earth's magnetism. Certainly the knowledge of this in Ireland was well attested. Corners were cut off houses if they stood in the way of fairy paths, or the doors and windows that covered the fairy paths had to be

---

9. "yn sleih veggey" in Manx, and "an bobel vyghan" in Cornish.

left open at night to let the fairies through. In Wales the Tylwyth Teg (fair folk) also had paths like those reserved for the Irish 'good people' and the Breton dead, and it was death to a mortal while walking in one of these paths if they met the fairy folk. On Man the Ronaldsway-Douglas road leads to the Fairy Bridge, where the traveller was (is) expected to stop the vehicle and acknowledge the fairies, or else an accident would ensue. There is a similar Fairy Bridge near Dunvegan on Skye, treated with reverence and fear by the locals and their horses because of its association with the little people and the legend of the fairy bride of the 4th Chief of the Macleods. In Co.Wexford in Ireland there is a fairy path that crossed a road near to the town of Ballysheog ("bally seighi" in Gaelic meaning 'the town of the fairies'). Although the spot is indistinguishable to the ordinary eye, nevertheless the locals would always stop there and acknowledge the fairies before they drove on.

In Cornwall a legend relates to St.Nuns Well (Piskey Well) near Pelynt which has a guardian elf and piskies that follow anyone who does not acknowledge them by leaving an offering. The power that the fairies have over certain paths and ways is manifested particularly in Cornwall in the idea of being piskey-led (also in Ireland, Wales and Brittany). For example Uter Bosence of Sancreed was piskey-led (led out of his way) at Botrea, and also attacked by sprights and spriggans and other strange apparitions (such as unearthly lights) that were seen hovering around the ruins of the old chapel. A cure for being piskey-led was to turn your coat (or glove) inside out, reversing the altered state of being you were in, to return to the normal world. Fairies are thus known to be very closely wedded to the land and to the idea of ancient paths and ways across the land. The other important factor is the time for connecting with them. In Scotland it was usually at twilight, the Celtic time between

the worlds. And the time of year was significant. In Man on 11th May (Old May Day's Eve) ["Oie Voaldyn" in Manx] the fairies were supposed to be particularly active. Fires were lit on hills to drive them away, a practice known about in other Celtic lands especially Cornwall, where on May Day and Midsummer Eve similar fires were lit to ward off evil spirits. So wherever you are in Celtic lands, keep a look-out for them for they can still be found, in Man swinging and playing in the tramman (elder) trees, in Wales dancing and singing on the mountain sides, in Scotland and Brittany pouring libations of milk over burial mounds at Samhain, in Ireland riding the horses and causing mischief, and in Cornwall dancing and frolicking in remote places in the land. The land is the domain of the fairies, they come from it, are a part of it and return to it. They are the spirit of the land, and as long as we believe the land has spirit, they have a place in our mythology.

Chapter Four

Piskey-led: Lost in the Mists of Time

"A man named Bottrell who lived near St.Teath was piskey-led at West Down, and when he turned his pockets inside out he heard the piskies going away laughing. Sometimes it is necessary to turn your coat inside out. A Zennor man said that to do the same thing with your socks or stockings is as good." [10]

Legends of the piskies or little-folk abound in Cornwall, and a very specific aspect of this is the notion of being piskey-led. To be piskey-led is to be led astray, to lose your way or your path, because the piskey-folk have somehow altered the familiar terrain, or in some mysterious way, the traveller's perception of it. This has relevance to studies of haunted highways, and/or paths of the dead running across the land, either visibly or invisibly. Jeremy Harte[11] has suggested that piskey-leading may be the development of three distinct types of tale: the mocking guide, the aimless wandering, and the deluded confinement. However, he also explores the possibility that it may be a

10. 'The Fairy Faith in Celtic Countries' – W.Y.Evans Wentz [OUP, 1911]

11. 'Pixie Leading' – Jeremy Harte [3rd Stone no.20, Spring 1995]

geophysical state: "It is tempting to see it as a product of certain localised physical energies, which will act on anyone coming within their field of force and lead to an altered state in which the core phenomenon, simple disorientation, is more or less elaborated according to cultural variables". In other words, the same anomalous geomagnetic energies at certain 'hot spots' in the land that can give rise to other visionary experiences (such as UFOs, ghosts, etc) can also lead to the experience of being piskey-led, when the belief in that phenomenon is widely accepted in the society, as it was in Cornwall-right up until the 19th century. If this theory has any credence, we should expect to find accounts of being piskey-led set in very specific parts of the landscape, and not in some vague no-man's land. Is this in fact what we find or not?

One of the best-known 'piskey-led' cases concerns one Uter Boscence who was led astray as he was returning from St.Just to Sancreed one evening after a hurling match.[12] When he got to the field at Bosence, called Parc-an-Chapel (the site of an old Celtic chapel) a cloud of fog rose from the moors, so thick that he could scarcely see a yard in front of him. He walked towards where he knew there was an opening in the field, but when he got there no opening was to be found. He tried to climb over the hedge, but the more he climbed the higher the hedge became. At the ruins of the old chapel, he saw "The most frightful sprights and spriggans one ever beheld" and encountered a demonic being that sent him "rolling down the field, tossed over the hedge, pushed through the brambles and furze, pitched over the bogs, and whirled away like dust before the wind." Now, the significance of this story is not only the place where it

---

12. 'Hearthside Stories of West Cornwall' – William Bottrell. Second Series [1873]

occurred (site of an old Celtic chapel) but also the time, it being midsummer night, the time of the old pagan festival, when bonfires were still lit on the hilltops. So we have here a doubly potent "between the worlds of time and space" setting for the experience to occur.

Places such as the old Celtic chapel of Boscence were often thought to be special places where one could encounter the Otherworld. In the story given above, the collector Bottrell says: "The ugliest of sprights and spriggans, with other strange apparitions, such as unearthly lights, were often seen hovering around the ruins of the old chapel."[13] Another collector Hunt[14] tells how an old man who got piskey-led in the area would often shelter at Caer Bran (Iron Age hillfort) "for everyone knew that anywhere within the Rings on Brane Hill, the same as at Bartinney, nothing evil that wanders the earth by night could harm them".

Another such place was "the green outside the gate at the end of Tresidder Lane" near St.Levan, a very specific location for another tale of piskey-leading. This green may have originally been a gathering place in ancient times; certainly some open spaces like this became known as special places. Hunt says that this green was a favourite place with the Small Folks to hold their fairs. A Mr Trezillian returning late one night from Penzance saw them and went to investigate. They were all over him like a swarm of bees, his horse ran off and he didn't know what to do "til by good luck he thought of what he had often heard, so he turned his glove inside out, threw it amongst the Small Folk, and ere the glove reached the ground they were all gone". He now had to find his horse, and the Small Folk, still determining to lead him astray,

13. 'Hearthside Stories of West Cornwall' – William Bottrell. Second Series [1873]

14. 'Popular Romances of the West of England' – Robert Hunt [1871]

bewildered him. He was piskie-led, and he could not find out where he was until broad daylight. Then he saw he was not a hundred yards from the place at which he had left his horse.

Mr Trezillian was returning from Penzance, and this illustrates the tendency of people to be piskey-led when they are going along everyday routes rather than being 'lost on the moors'. For example, an old man named Classen was piskey-led one bright moonlit night: "He was returning to Ludgvan from Gulval, but no matter which path he took it led him back to where he had started. At last he turned his coat inside out, the only way to break the spell, and reached Ludgvan without further trouble"

Another tale which has great geo-mythic significance is the legend of Pee Tregeer (An Pee), who was able to see a fairy at Penzance market due to her illicit use of a "greenish ointment". The tale[15] is very specific about the route she took back from Penzance to Pendeen: "She didn't return by way of Polteggan Bottom and Boswednan, though it's the nearest... she took her course through Castle Horneck fields". After three of four miles she begins to enter what we would call a state of altered consciousness "being so distracted she couldn't tell whether she was going up hill or down dale half the way". She has a vision of a man on horseback which metamorphoses into a cross, meets a piskey thresher at Boslow, and finally on the Gump near Cam Kenidjack is piskey-led, encountering amongst other things little folk with a goblet in the shape of a poppy capsule. Devereux & Weatherhill[16] suggest that this is an opium reference, and that would certainly fit with the notion of the event occurring

---

15. 'Hearthside Stories of West Cornwall' – William Bottrell. Second Series [1873]

16. 'Myths and legends of Cornwall' - Paul Devereux & Craig Weatherhill' [Sigma, 1994]

in a state of altered consciousness. They also make the point that the route An Pee takes is a specific geomythic path across the landscape. It is also an event, like the Uter Boscence one, that occurs at a time outside of time, namely the eve of Halloween (the old Celtic festival of Samhain). In addition, to further reinforce the point, she has a vision on The Gump of the Little People celebrating Beltane with maypole and garlands. So An Pee has been transported in time by exactly half-a-year to the mirror-image pagan Celtic spring festival. The tale thus contains all the elements that link it to a time and space before and beyond the present: a visionary experience that occurs by taking narcotics, in which the veils between the worlds disappear and An Pee moves freely between this world and the Otherworld. She gains entry into this Otherworld by taking a specific mythic route across the land.

One tale[17] that illustrates the protagonist moving through time is that of John Sturtridge who, when walking home to Luxulyan, meets a party of Little People at Tregarden Down. He becomes piskey-led: "The Down, well known from early experience, became like ground untrodden, and after a long trial no gate or stile was to be found". In this case, he not only becomes disoriented, but is transported many miles away to the beach at Par, where he is led to the wine cellar of Squire Tremaine. He is found the next morning, and sentenced to hang for his misdemeanour, but at his execution a "little lady" appears (one of the piskie-folk in disguise) and with a shout of "Ho and away to France" he is once again transported through time to effect his escape. Here we have perhaps a late memory of some ritual formula or incantation that was used by ancient

---

17. From 'Popular Romances of the West of England' – Robert Hunt [1871]

peoples to "time-travel", that is, go on shamanic journeys to the spirit world. As we have seen, many of these piskey-led tales contain elements that hint of such earlier ritual and shamanic practices.

Another similar tale of altered consciousness comes from the Rev. Baring-Gould, writing about Parson Hawker, the Vicar of Morwenstow in 1876.[18] He tells the story of a man returning home from market and passing between dense hedges, who saw a light and heard music and singing. Looking through the hedge, he saw an elf sitting on a toadstool, holding a lantern formed from a campanula flower, from which poured a greenish-blue light. A group of fairies was dancing in a ring. The man described what he did: "I looked and listened a while, and then I got quietly hold of a great big stone and heaved it up, and I dreshed in amongst them all, and then I up on my horse and galloped away as hard as I could, and never drew rein until I came home to Morwenstow. Next day I went back to the spot, and there lay the stone, just where I had dreshed it".

Many of the elements of the 'transported in time' motif are here: the man following a prescribed route home, "between tall hedges" and thus deprived of landscape features, seeing a light, having a vision, which included the fairy with a flower that gave off an ethereal other-worldly light, and then returning to see nothing there. Janet Bord speculates[19] that the man may have come under the influence of some electro-magnetic energy which caused him to see the fairies who were really there, the lantern being the light from the power source. Or alternatively, he may have hallucinated the elf and the dancing fairies when he came

---

18. 'The Vicar of Morwenstow' – S.Baring Gould [1876]

19. 'Fairies: real encounters with little people' – Janet Bord [Michael O'Mara Books, 1997]

under the influence of an electro-magnetic discharge.

Finally, if such journeys through space and time existed in earlier days and were still being written about in disguised form in the 19th century, have they altogether disappeared in our "age of reason"? Katherine Briggs suggests not. She recounts[20] a story recorded in 1961 which tells of a woman who went to a house in Cornwall to do some secretarial work. When the farm came into sight she walked in and asked if she were on the right track to the Manor. She was given careful directions, but couldn't find the second white gate to go through. "I had a most creepy feeling. I went all along the hedge but there was only one gate. Then somebody came up the bridle track whistling, and the thick mist cleared and there was no hedge. It was one of the farm lads sent after me who knew what to do. 'Here's your white gate, Miss' he said, and, sure enough, there it was beside the other one."

I also have a tale from my personal experience. One night a group of us went up to the top of Bartinney Hill to celebrate one of the festivals. When we had finished (about midnight) we started to come down, but became totally lost and disorientated. We blundered about for a while until we were getting quite desperate. Then one of us (who happened to be a Bard of the Cornish Gorsedd) said: "We've been piskey-led. Anyone with change in their pocket, turn it over." Several of us did, and immediately we found ourselves on the correct path and made our way to the bottom of the hill, where, an examination of our watches showed the time to be 4am! Were we piskey-led on that night that lay between the worlds? We should never underestimate the power of the Otherworld: it still lies all around us today.

20. 'The Fairies in tradition and literature' – Katherine Briggs [Routledge, 1967]

Chapter Five

The Cornish Otherworld

As we have seen, most Celtic literature and myth has the concept of an 'Otherworld': in Irish it was known as 'Aes Sidhe' and in Welsh folklore Annwfyn or Annwn (pronounced 'annoon'). This 'Otherworld' had many other names and manifestations, including the Tir-na-nog "The Land of Youth", Tir-innambeo - "The Land of the Living", Tir Tairngirc "The Land of Promise", and Tir N-aill "The Other World". It was also thought to consist of the Upperworld, the Middle World and the Underworld, and in many stories it is the place occupied by the ancestors. Often the hero goes in search of the ancient dead, as it is they who remember and preserve the traditions of older times. However, the Otherworld generally is not a place of doom and gloom. Rather than an ending of life, the Otherworld of the Celts is a gateway into another kind of life. Often this life looks very much like our everyday life, though it is transformed by its beauty and by the Otherworldly creatures who inhabit it. It is in fact a "magical idealised mirror image of the human world." [21]

The creatures who inhabit this world include the dead ancestors, but also gods, spirits, supernatural creatures and strange beasts, and often the fairy folk. The place of the Otherworld is also a place out of time: time moves at a different pace and if an ordinary mortal enters the Otherworld he or she does not grow any older there. However, if she or he then returns to the everyday world, time has passed and all his or her companions have grown older. Other common elements in the Welsh and Irish stories include the passage into the Otherworld, which is often into a burial mound or "fairy mound', or across or under water. Also the time for entering the Otherworld is often at the Celtic festivals, when the boundaries between the earthly and supernatural worlds is broken down and spirits and humans can move freely between the two lands. Well-known stories that feature voyages to the Otherworld include 'The Voyage of Bran' from the Irish mythic cycle, and 'Pwyll, Lord of Dyfed' from the Welsh *Mabinogian*. Pwyll. Lord of Dyfed, spends a year in the Otherworld, and there are many other lesser-known stories from myth and folklore that include the same themes and accounts.

If the Otherworld plays such an important part in the stories of other Celtic nations, the question arises as to whether there was a Cornish equivalent of the realm. The nearest equivalent to the Welsh 'Annwyn' is the Cornish word 'annown' and there is also the Cornish word 'ankow'

---

21. C.f 'Dictionary of Celtic Myth and Legend' – Miranda Green (Thames & Hudson, 1998), 'Tales of the Celtic Underworld' – John Matthews (Blandford, 1998) & 'Celtic Myth and Legend' – Mike Dixon-Kennedy (Blandford, 1996)

meaning a personification of death. 'Annown" as a word seems to have been constructed by analogy from Breton & Welsh, meaning a personification of death. 'Annown" as a word, but 'ankow' is a native word, found in Old, Middle and Late Cornish with up to 30 occurrences in texts including 'The Creation of the World' (1611). References to the Otherworld also occur in *The Fairy Faith in Celtic Countries*, where Evans-Wenz says: "The Celtic Otherworld is like that hidden realm of subjectivity lying just beyond the horizon of mortal existence, which we cannot behold when we would, save with the mystic vision of the [Celtic] seer".[22] He points out that all Celtic nations have their mythic islands off-shore which were often thought to be the dwelling-place of the Otherworld: In Brittany it was called Ys; in Wales it was known as Caer Arianrhod; in Ireland various names including Hy Brasil; and in Cornwall of course the lost land of Lyonesse. There was also a legend that the Isles of Scilly were the place of the dead, where souls went after death to rest. In Welsh myth (such as the stories of 'Culhwch and Olwen' and 'Branwen. Daughter of Llyr') "Cornwall" often becomes a metaphor for a kind of Celtic Otherworld to where Arthur chases a boar and disappears into the sea, and where Bran's men open a door to the land and come face to face with all their grief.

It is however the stories recorded by both Robert Hunt and William Bottrcll in the late 19th Century that perhaps furnish us with the best folkloric evidence of the concept of an Otherworld in Cornwall. One of the most powerful of these stories is one recorded by Bottrcll as 'Fairy Dwelling on Selena Moor'.[23] The story concerns the disappearance

---

22. 'The Fairy Faith in Celtic Countries' – W.Y.Evans Wentz [OUP, 1911]
23. 'Hearthside Stories of West Cornwall' – William Bottrell. Second Series [1873]

of a farmer William Noy, and how, after three days, he is discovered apparently asleep on a stretch of boggy ground near Selena moor. When he comes to he tells a strange story of taking a short cut across the moor and getting lost in a part of the moor he had never seen before. After wandering many miles, he heard strains of music and spied lights glimmering. He then saw hundreds of Little People, amongst whom was one Grace Hutchens, who had formerly been his sweetheart until she had died 3 or 4 years before. She had in fact been abducted by the Fairie Folk, all of whom were originally mortals who had lived thousands of years ago. This makes explicit the nature of the Otherworld as the dwelling place of ghosts of prehistoric people. The Otherworld is also described by Grace Hutchens as a "beautiful garden with alleys all bordered by roses and many sweet flowers that she had never seen the light of. Apples and other tempting fruit dropped in the walks and hung overhead, bursting ripe." Significantly the garden is also described as being surrounded by trees and water, indicative of a liminal boundary between this world and the Otherworld. And perhaps most significantly of all, the Fairy Folk are described as "not of our religion but star-worshippers", perhaps a memory of the pagan beliefs of the Ancestors. Grace also speaks of being able to take the form of any bird she pleases, and shape-shifting was also a common Celtic motif.

The road to the Otherworld through caves and mounds, so typical of Irish and Welsh tales, may also be found in the Cornish story of the young farmer Richard Vingoe, who follows a path into an underground passage on Treville Cliffs and, on emerging, finds himself in a "strange pleasant-looking country" that is Fairyland. Here he too meets his former lover who has been dead a few years, and in this case she leads him back to the Upper World by a shorter road through an opening in a cam. In another story, the Lost Child of St.Allen,[24] a young child is taken to the Other World by being lured by some beautiful music that leads him to the centre of a dark grove. A passage appears before him as if made by some invisible being, and he finds himself on the edge of a small lake. He falls asleep, which is the prelude to crossing the liminal threshold between this world and the Otherworld. He is then taken "by a beautiful lady through palaces of the most gorgeous description". "Pillars of glass supported arches which glistened with every colour and there were hung with crystals far exceeding anything which were ever seen in the caverns of a Cornish mine". Eventually, he is restored to the everyday world. This story includes many of the elements found in the Welsh and Irish annals: the beautiful music leading to the Otherworld, the place surrounded by a lake or at the bottom of a lake, and the beautiful state of the Land itself.

Although the stories of the Cornish Otherworld are never specifically described as "the Otherworld", it is clear that this is what they are. In the story of 'Cherry of Zennor'[25] for example, there are a number of important trigger words in the story to indicate that the reader is on a journey to the Otherworld. Cherry

---

24. From 'Popular Romances of the West of England' – Robert Hunt [1871]

25. From 'Popular Romances of the West of England' – Robert Hunt [1871]

meets a "gentleman" at a *cross roads* (a magical place of transformation), and he takes her on a journey through lanes where "sweet briars and honeysuckles perfumed the air, and the reddest of ripe apples hung from the trees over the lane". The fecundity of nature where everything grows abundantly is always a hint that we are on the way to the Otherworld. Then they come to a "stream of water as clear as crystal, which ran across the lane" where the man carries her across. Streams and rivers are usually liminal places, marking the division between this world and the Otherworld. Having crossed the stream, they arrived at a garden where everything was more intensely beautiful than anything in the everyday world. "Flowers of every dye were around her; fruits of all kinds hung above her; and the birds, sweeter of song than any she had ever heard, burst out into a chorus of rejoicing". Cherry was then taken into a house which was "yet more beautiful". "Flowers of every kind grew everywhere, and the sun seemed to shine everywhere, and yet she did not see the sun". Cherry spends some time in this enchanted land, looking after the house and the Master's child, but it is no ordinary place. One room contains people who have been turned to stone, and Cherry has some ointment put on her eyes which gives her the gift of seeing the Fairy Folk. Eventually she returns to the "real world" but is forever changed by the experience.

Stories such as these seem to contain aspects which link them back to a far earlier time than when they were written down, a time of the early sagas and stories from other Celtic lands such as Ireland and Brittany, full of strange events and journeys to Other Realms. The Otherworld was ever present for the Celts, and can be found as strongly in these Cornish stories as anywhere in the classic Celtic literature.

Chapter Six

Celtic Totem Animals

The Celtic peoples were deeply connected to the natural world and the animals they encountered[26] there. The beasts of the fields and forests, the birds in the air, the insects and reptiles of the earth, and the fishes of the seas were thought of as not only inhabiting this mundane world, but also as being mediators between this world and the Otherworld. Animals were thought of as being older than humankind and therefore nearer to the gods, and were seen as having their counterparts in the spirit world, to where the shamans would travel to meet them as 'spirit guides'. Therefore animals became teachers from whom humans could learn and obtain information, so that their appearance in the mundane world was thought of as presaging some insight or supernatural occurrence. This connection between the world of the gods and goddesses and the world of animals is vividly illustrated in the panel from the

---

26. The inspiration for this chapter came from the late Gloria Falconbridge, with whom I worked on the material.

1stC BCE Gundestrup Cauldron *[shown below]* that depicts the Celtic horned God Cernunnos holding a serpent and surrounded by an array of animals, each one of which would have represented some spiritual force or significance.

Many stories would have been told about the relationship between humans and this mythological/spiritual realm of animals, and so when these tales came to be written down by the Christian monks, they rationalised the role of these animals to a more down-to-earth function. However, the tales still convey the power of the myth that holds within itself the significance of the animals on a spiritual level, and by scratching the surface of some of these tales (such as the Welsh Mabinogi, the Irish mythic cycle and early Arthurian legend) we can get a glimpse of the Celtic world of animal forms and powers, a world that still lives on in the subconscious of all of us today. In Cornwall, a rich source of material for the significance of these animals can be found in the collections of tales by William Bottrell & Robert Hunt, written down in the late 19th century, but doubtless originally dating back to much earlier times, perhaps to the Celtic era itself.

Reverence for animals is as old as humanity itself. An altar to a bear (deity?) was discovered at Drachenloch cave in Switzerland dating back to c.40,000 BCE, and in many of the caves of central Europe, paintings dating from the Upper Paleolithic Period (30,000-18,000 BCE) depict animals such as bears, horses and bisons. These paintings are thought of as having been made by shamans in contact with the spirit world, so the animals depicted may be considered to be mediators between the animal and spirit worlds. The depiction of Cernunnos on the Gundestrup Cauldron wearing antler horns finds a parallel in the discovery of antlers intended for wearing at Star Carr in Yorkshire. When dated, these antlers were found to have been used as long ago as 7500 BCE.

Many Celtic tribes were named after animals, or had animals as totems for their tribe. Examples include the Epidii ('horse-people'), the Orcoi ('boar-people'), the Taurisci ('bull-people') and the Brannovices ('raven-people'). The leaders of these Iron-Age tribes were often considered to have animal characteristics and qualities: for example King Mark of Cornwall supposedly had horse's ears, an Irish chieftan had cat's ears, and again in Cornwall the ruler Rialobranus is named after the bird the 'Royal Raven'. In many of the Irish & Welsh mythic stories, animals and birds appear at significant moments in the tales, often as messengers from the Otherworld. In the Welsh *Tale of Culhwch and Olwen* (first written down in the 11thC CE but with material dating to a much earlier period), Culhwch has to enlist the help of supernatural animals, which include the Blackbird of Kilgowry, the Eagle of Gwernabwy, the Stag of Rhedenure, and the Salmon of Llyn Llyw. There are elements of shape-shifting between human and animal forms in the tale: Culhwch takes on the mantle of a pig, and is subsequently linked with a transformed boar, and the Mabon (the divine hunter son of the Mother Goddess) appears in the form of a wren.

In the story of *Pwyll, Prince of Dyfed*, Pwyll has a close association with the supernatural right at the beginning of the tale. While out hunting he sees a pack of strange white hounds that pursue and overcome a most beautiful white stag. These animals are from the Otherworld, and are followed by Arawn himself, king of Annwn, the Welsh Otherworld. Later in the tale, Pwyll encounters a woman on a horse, whom he can never catch, despite using his swiftest steeds. She turns out to be Rhiannon, "divine Queen", a Celtic horse Goddess, related to the Gaulish horse-Goddess Epona. In all these cases, the appearance of animals - hounds, stag, horse - denote that the threshold between this world and the Otherworld is about to be crossed. And finally, there is the tale of the poet and bard Taliesen, in which the boy Gwion Bach accidentally swallows three drops from the Goddess Ceridwen's cauldron. He receives her gifts of inspiration and wisdom that she had intended for her son Afagddu, so she pursues him. In order to escape, he turns into a hare, so she becomes a greyhound. He becomes a fish, so she turns into an otter. He then becomes a bird, so she turns into a hawk. Finally he becomes a grain of wheat, so she becomes a hen and swallows him. Nine months later she gives birth to Taliesen. Later in life, Taliesen claims that he has been a buck, a wild sow, a speckled cat and a goat during his life. Clearly here we are seeing a Celtic world of shape-shifting and embodiment of animals in a kind of shamanic way, relating to the great cycles of birth, life, death and rebirth. These animals stand at the gates of both worlds - this world and the spirit Otherworld.

HORSES ⚘

Horses appear time and again in Celtic myth and, as well as being symbols of power and possessions, very often represent the realm of the Celtic Otherworld. The

Celtic horse Goddess was worshipped as the White Mare, known in Gaul as Epona (*Epo* is Gallic for 'horse'), in Wales as Rhiannon and in Ireland as Macha. As Epona, she is sometimes accompanied by a dog, symbolising her Underworld aspect. She was worshipped as a deity of fertility, war, sovereignty and happiness in the afterlife. In the story of Rhiannon, not only does she appear riding on a white mare, but later in the story, she is forced into carrying visitors to the King's palace on her back. In the story of Macha, the Goddess Macha was forced to race against the fastest horses in Ireland while she was pregnant. She died at the winning post while giving birth to twins, and cursed all Ulstermen as a result. All these stories portray the horse Goddess as coming from, and returning to, the Otherworld, and horses were revered as being able to travel between the two worlds. They opened the gates of life at Beltane, and carried the souls of the dead back to the Underworld at Samhain.

A memory of this appears in some of the Cornish tales. In the story of the Giants of Towednack[27], the enchanter Pengersec rides a 'demon-steed' "which seems to tread the air and spurn the ground - no animal of flesh and blood". In the story of One-Eyed Joan[28] a spirit-horse appears and takes Joan on a wild ride across Clodgey Moor. In the tale of the Fairy Dwelling on Selena Moor[29], a horse takes its own path and leads Mr.Noy to an enchanted Otherworld. And for shape-shifting stories, the wise woman or white

---

27. 'Hearthside Stories of West Cornwall' – William Bottrell. First Series [1870]

28. 'Hearthside Stories of West Cornwall' – William Bottrell. First Series [1870]

29. 'Hearthside Stories of West Cornwall' – William Bottrell. Second Series [1873]

witch of Treen changes into a horse, and in A Night's Ride to Scilly[30] the devil appears in the form of a horse and takes Jackey to the Scillies. Shape-shifting witches hark back to pre-Christian shamankas, and the devil of course is only a Christian name for a pagan god or spirit being.

COWS & BULLS ⚜

Closely following on from horses, cattle are a very important symbol of wealth and power, commemorated in the epic poem *The Cattle Raid of Cooley* and collected in the ancient Irish manuscript (c.1106 CE) *The Book of the Dun Cow*. To the Celts, the cow symbolised the sacredness of motherhood with the milk representing the life force itself. Milk from a sacred cow was an early form of communion with the Goddess. The Goddess/Saint Bridget was nourished by a cow who came from the Otherworld, with white body and red ears, and she is often depicted milking a cow (such as in the carving on the tower on Glastonbury Tor). This motif of the supernatural nourishment of the cow can be found in the Cornish tale of Tom the Giant-killer[31], who lived with his wife Joan at Towednack. Their children were reported to be weaned by "suckling the cows and goats ... which took their sucklings as naturally as if they had been their own calves and kids". Piskies were also known to milk a cow[32]. A supernatural cow belonging to the Little People also appears in the tale 'The Small People's Cow'[33]. She gives twice as

---

30. *ibid*

31. 'Hearthside Stories of West Cornwall' – William Bottrell. First Series [1870]

32. From 'Popular Romances of the West of England' – Robert Hunt [1871]

33. 'Hearthside Stories of West Cornwall' – William Bottrell. Second Series [1873]

much milk as an ordinary cow, and also feeds the fairies as well, who appear one Midsummer's Night to milk her. Cattle were driven between fires to purify them in all Celtic lands including Cornwall at Beltane, and it was considered very unlucky not to do so.

Closely linked to cows are bulls. In the Celtic world, the bull is often associated with deities of poetry, healing and the Underworld. It features strongly in Ireland's creation mythology, and in one story, St. Patrick kills a bull by trickery, which then miraculously returns to life. In a Cornish story, two tinners visit the hill-top territory of the giant Denbras[34] and see a young boy and girl mounted on a young bull, riding it back to back. They may be thought of as having entered the Otherworld, and seeing some ancient rite, perhaps one that is a memory of bull-leaping contests in Minoan Crete. In an article in MM28 p.9-11, Brendan McMahon has suggested[35] that Jack the Tinkeard, who features in the same tale, takes on the role of a shamanic figure in his association with the bull and his coat which is made out of black bull's hide. In the story of the 'Devil's Money'[36] the devil himself appears in the form of a bull.

DEERS 🦌

Deers are frequent visitors in the Celtic stories, and very often appear to lead people in and out of the Otherworld. The Tuatha de Danaan, shapeshifting Irish otherworldly folk, appeared to people in the form of a White Doe or White Stag, and led people deeper into the woods to encounter

---

34. 'Hearthside Stories of West Cornwall' – William Bottrell. First Series [1870]

35. 'A Cornish Shaman' – Brendan McMahon [Meyn Mamvro, no.28]

36. 'Hearthside Stories of West Cornwall' – William Bottrell. Second Series [1873]

the Otherworld. In the story of Pwyll, it is a white stag who leads Pwyll to encounter Arawn, Lord of the Underworld. One of the Irish hero Fionn's Otherworldly wives, Sadbh, was said to have been turned into a fawn by a druid, but may originally have been the Irish Deer Goddess of the same name. And the horned God Cernunnos, the Lord of the Forest, was depicted as an anthropomorphized stag.

There is a very interesting Cornish tale[37] about Robert, Earl of Cornwall, who, while out hunting one day chases an elusive red deer deep into the forest (the Otherworld?). He then has an encounter with a black goat and sees an apparition of his friend William Rufus on its back. The goat says it is an "evil spirit" taking Rufus "to judgement". Later Robert discovers that at the very moment of the vision, Rufus had been slain in the New Forest by an arrow. This story has both deer and goat linked to the Otherworld.

PIGS & BOARS ૱

In Celtic mythology boars are token animals of strength and power: according to Anne Ross they were "without doubt the cult animal *par excellence* of the Celts"[38], and the boar was the national symbol of the Gauls. Pigs were revered as the sacred animal of Mother Earth, and were thought of as coming from the Underworld, so were considered as guides for shamanic journeys. In Irish myth, Medb's nephews eluded her in the form of swine. In Wales, the Goddess Cerridwen was called 'the great white sow', and her Underworld cauldron was the place where all souls had to return for inspiration and regeneration. She was a shapeshifter and an Underworld initiator. In another story the *Twrch Trwyth* a magical transformed pig swims across

---

37. From 'Popular Romances of the West of England' – Robert Hunt [1871]

38. 'Pagan Celtic Britain' – Anne Ross [Routledge, 1967]

the sea from Ireland, and is then hunted by (King) Arthur into Cornwall, the far west that probably represents the land of the dead. A legend in Sancreed in West Penwith tells how St.Creda was transformed into a swineherd after accidently killing his father, and a carving above the entrance to the Church depicts him holding a pig.

WOLVES & DOGS 🐾

A wolf appears as the companion of Cernunnos on the Gundestrup cauldron. Because they hunted at night in the dark, wolves were thought of as useful spirit guides for shamanic journeys. St. Ruan, who has a church and holy well dedicated to him on the Lizard peninsula, had, according to his tales, a particularly close affinity with wolves, and while in Brittany was accused of being one in disguise. He seems to have been a shamanic shape-shifter of a saint. Dogs were also connected to the Otherworld and thought of as chthonic animals. They were totem animals of roads, trackways and crossroads, and stood at threshold places as guardians and protectors. The Irish hero Finn mac Cool had, as his companions, two hounds of semi-human origin. Later, probably because of their association with pagan Gods and heroes, hounds came to be viewed as the companions of the Devil, who would ride out with them in his Wild Hunt. In the Cornish story 'Dando and his Dogs'[39] the indulgent priest of St.Germans is out hunting with his dogs and taken by the Devil down to the River Lynher, where he disappears, presumably to hell, the Christian Underworld.

HARES & CATS 🐾

Hares and cats were sacred to the Celts. Just before she began her campaign against the Romans, Queen Boudica

---

39. 'Popular Romances of the West of England' – Robert Hunt [1871]

of the Iceni released a hare while invoking the Goddess Andraste. And in Ireland, there was a cult of the sacred cat, evidenced by The Cave of the Cats at Rathcroghan, an underground souterrain that was the entrance to the Otherworld; and the oracular cave shrine at Clough in Connaught whose prophetess was "a slender black cat reclining on a chair of old silver". Later, both animals came to be thought of as familiars to witches and wise women. They appear frequently in the Cornish tales. For example, in the story of Betty Stoggs[40] a cat leads Betty to her stolen baby; and in the Witch of Treva a hare and a cat were familiars or spirits of the witch and both appeared at her death[41]. In other stories there are hares that no dog can chase, and in one story[42] the hares shape-shift into Mag the Witch. In the story of Duffy and the Devil[43] Squire Lovell chases a hare into Boleigh fogou and finds a coven of witches; in The Legend of Pengersec, a white hare, who is the spirit of a murdered woman, frightens off dogs and wolves[44]; in Laying Wild Harris's Ghost hares were kept as familiars by the Rev.Polkinhorne[45]; and in The White Hare, a broken-hearted maiden comes back in the shape of a hare.[46]

---

40. 'Hearthside Stories of West Cornwall' – William Bottrell. Second Series [1873]

41. 'Popular Romances of the West of England' – Robert Hunt [1871]

42. 'Hearthside Stories of West Cornwall' – William Bottrell. First Series [1870]

43. 'Hearthside Stories of West Cornwall' – William Bottrell. Second Series [1873]

44. *ibid*

45. 'Hearthside Stories of West Cornwall – William Bottrell. Third Series [1880]

46. 'Popular Romances of the West of England' – Robert Hunt [1871]

BIRDS ⚶

Birds were especially sacred to the Celts, in particular the eagle, raven, hawk, owl, crane, goose and swan. In the Cornish tale of Grace Hutchings[47], her dead spirit could take the form of any bird. In the Welsh tale of Blodewedd, she is turned into the form of an **owl**, and linked to death and the Underworld. In the Cornish tale of Mr.Lenine of Tregonebris[48] it is said that Betty Foss was a witch, and, unusually, an owl was her familiar. An owl comes to listen to Jack the Tinkeard as he played his harp[49], and both owls and **choughs** call Tom's name later in the same tale as a presage of death. It was thought that King Arthur could appear in the form of a chough or a **raven**[50], and it is said that the croaking of a raven over a house bodes evil to some member of the family. In all these cases the birds are seen as embodied spirits or emissaries from the Otherworld. In the Irish stories, the triple Goddess of death, the Morrighan, appears as a battle crow, and in one of her aspects as the Goddess Badhbd, her name means 'raven' or 'crow'. The Celtic God Bran's name also means 'raven', and is remembered in Cornwall at Caer Bran hilltop site, Brane village, and St.Breward on Bodmin Moor (from 'Branwalder' = raven lord). **Magpies** also were thought of as supernatural birds bringing good or bad luck. Magpies from the Otherworld were able to converse with humans. A

---

47. 'Hearthside Stories of West Cornwall' – William Bottrell. Second Series [1873]

48. 'Popular Romances of the West of England' – Robert Hunt [1871]

49. 'Hearthside Stories of West Cornwall' – William Bottrell. First Series [1870]

50. 'Popular Romances of the West of England' – Robert Hunt [1871]

magpie talked to Joan the Giantess[51], and in the story of Margaret the white witch of Zennor[52] she talks to all manner of creatures, including magpies, hares, a goat and a cat, who come to her.

Finally, a few rather special birds should be mentioned. The **cuckoo** does not appear in the Celtic myths, but there is much folklore surrounding this strange bird. One Cornish story[53] tells of how the folk of Towednack have no patron saint and try to hedge in a cuckoo. Although this is told as a tale to show up the simplicity of the Towednack folk, it may in fact be a distant folk memory of the pre-Christian origin of the Celtic saints, who were close to nature and the seasons, and a deep-rooted belief that people could be transformed into bird shapes. Certainly, the crane (no longer native to Britain) carries this association: the son of the God Manannan had a mistress Aoife who was turned into a **crane**, and her skin was used to make a crane bag, a receptacle for shamanic bards to carry. And the **swan** appears in many Celtic tales, sometimes associated with the Goddess/Saint Bridget. In the Irish legend of the Tale of Lir, Lir's wife Aoibh bore Lir four children, who were subsequently magically changed into swans by his second wife. The swan can often represent the transition of the soul through states of being and states of enchantment.

All these birds and animals were important to the Celts, not just for what they represented in themselves,

---

51. 'Hearthside Stories of West Cornwall' – William Bottrell. First Series [1870]

52. *ibid*

53. 'Hearthside Stories of West Cornwall – William Bottrell. Third Series [1880]

but also as visitors from the Otherworld, and as helpers, teachers and protectors, leading humankind to spiritual growth and enlightenment.

Chapter Seven

Mermaids and Sea Goddesses

Less than two hundred years ago, the 'West Briton' newspaper on 6th July 1827 described sightings of mermaids, up to five of them, over three days, in and around a cavern on the beach at Mawgan Porth, after a young man entered the cavern and encountered something in human shape with long hair hanging about it. Between the worlds, at the threshold of the tides, crossing the space between the human race and the other-worldly watery realms, swim the mermaids. In Cornwall they are known from various places, and they are powerful creatures not to be trifled with. No pretty-pretty beauty queens, sitting preening themselves on the rocks, the Cornish mermaids can control the wild seas and influence human destiny. For example, at Lamorna in West Cornwall the mermaid would sit on the rocks and sing plaintively before bad weather and a shipwreck. At Seaton in East Cornwall the mermaid silted up the harbour when a local man insulted her. And the same story is told of Padstow. Here the harbour was once deep and open, a veritable playground for mermaids; but one day a man shot at her with a gun, and the mermaid in anger silted up the harbour entrance with the Doom Bar.

Mermaids also had the ability to bewitch and lure men away from the mortal world. They were other-worldly shape-shifters who could appear and disappear with the tides. At Cury on the Lizard, an old man named Luty found a mermaid stranded on the rocks by the receding tide. Luty took pity on her and carried her back to the sea, and she granted him three wishes in return. He chose not gold and silver, but the power to do good to his neighbours, and in particular to break the spells of witchcraft, to charm away diseases, and (in one version[54]) to discover thieves and restore stolen goods (and in another[55]) to have these powers continue in his family for ever. These powers having been given, Hunt says that to his day: "A family well-known in Cornwall have for some generations exercised the power of charming, etc." As she slips away into the waves, the mermaid called Morvena tries to persuade Luty to go with her and see her wonderful sea caverns. He is tempted by her words and almost in her power, but he remembers his home at the last moment and breaks free. However, nine years later to the day she comes for him while he is out fishing, and he swims off into the sea with her, never to be seen again. Mermaids represent the Otherworld, the same world as inhabited by the fairies and piskies, and as such they are the spirits of the world of Faery, a world no longer generally believed in, but accepted as just as real as our own in the past, especially in rural areas like Cornwall.

The most famous Cornish mermaid legend is that of Zennor. It is, like the Cury legend, one of an otherworldly creature who tempts away a mortal man. In this legend, the mermaid appears at the back of the church in the guise of

54. 'Popular Romances of the West of England' – Robert Hunt [1871]
55. 'Hearthside Stories of West Cornwall' – William Bottrell. First Series [1870]

a beautiful woman with an exquisite voice. She falls in love with Matthew Trewella, the churchwarden's son and finest choirboy in Zennor. One day he slips away with her down towards the sea and the pair are never seen again, except when the captain of a ship passing by has an encounter with the mermaid. The legend is commemorated in a carving on the dark holly-oak wood of the chancel seat in Zennor church, a most unusual thing to find in a Christian church (although a wall painting at Breage church near Helston also depicts a mermaid). Even more unusual, the plaque on the wall above the seat makes the suggestion that mermaids were originally pagan goddesses of the sea. The legend of Zennor church is interesting in this respect. Its patron saint is St.Senara, originally a pagan princess Asenora of Brittany. She was cast adrift on the sea in a barrel when she was pregnant until she was washed up on the coast of Ireland, from where she returned to Brittany via Cornwall, and founded the church at Zennor. Mermaid, saint and sea-goddess all seem inextricably intertwined, and may all be aspects of an other-world sea-goddess who was later Christianised.

Along the coast, the tiny hamlet of Morvah may itself be named after *Morvech, which has links with a Breton word meaning sea-maidens or sea-daughters. Certainly mermaids in Cornwall were originally called mere-maids or merrymaids, and Ian Cooke[56] has pointed out that they were identified in folklore with the moon and the Goddess of love (Aphrodite) who may have shape-shifted into a fish-tail as an aid to her escape from the attentions of the pursuing sun-god. The linking of the moon and the tides is of course well-known, and the identification of mermaids with the moon is further

---

56. 'Journey to the Stones' – Ian McNeil Cooke [Mên-an-Tol Studio, 1987 & 1996]

strengthened by her attendant iconography of a mirror and a comb, found almost universally in mermaid depictions. The mirror may originally have represented the full moon, and the comb the phases of the moon. The African goddess Mami Watu is depicted with a comb and a mirror, and there is also a very interesting carving on a 15th century chancel arch in Clonfert Abbey in Co.Galway in the west of Ireland depicting a mermaid carrying a mirror and decorated with a circular object in her vaginal area, that may be a moon or a sun symbol. This semi sheila-na-gig combines notions of the sea, the moon, and Goddess sexuality.

Clonfert Abbey lies beside the River Shannon, named after a Goddess Sinaan, and is a reminder that not all mermaids are goddesses of the sea. Most rivers and lakes also had their tutelary goddess in ancient times. They were not tolerated under Christianity, but could not be quite eliminated, especially if they were very powerful, so went underground, or in this case under the sea or river. For example, in Herefordshire at Marden, a mermaid is said to live in the River Lugg beside the church. She possessed the church bell which she kept under the water, and attempts to steal it back from her all failed. In Staffordshire a mermaid dwelt on the high moors above Buxton and Leek in Doxey's Pool and Black Mere. When an attempt was made to drain Black Mere in the 19thC, she once again appeared to warn that if her pool dried up she would drown Leek. Nearby is the river Dane, probably named after the Celtic goddess Danu, so these stories are all telling of the conflict between Christianity and/or 'progress' and the older and more elemental pagan Goddess religion. The Goddesses of the Old Religion shape-shifted into saints, giantesses and mermaids under the new.

Belief in mermaids was therefore not just a silly fancy by a credulous people. It was rooted in an ancient belief and tradition, a respect for the power of the sea or dangerous rivers and lakes, and a subconscious awareness that the world of spirit was closer to the world of mankind than we some-times might like to pretend. The sirens of the sea who in Greek myth could hire men away to magic islands and strange worlds still have the ability to call us from this world to the Other World that lies just beyond the horizon of the sea, and sometimes washes up on our shores with the mermaids.

Chapter Eight

Faces in the Rocks, Spirits in the Stones

It is generally acknowledged nowadays that to ancient peoples natural stones, rocks and tors were thought to contain the dwelling places of spirits, often spirits of the departed ancestors. In *Spirits of the Rocks*[57] archaeologists Dick Cole & Andy M. Jones say: "People are likely to have regarded the landscape as being the creation of spirits, gods or ancestors, and it is likely that stories, myths and legends would have grown up around landscape features. Significant natural features may have been considered to be the homes of spirits, ancestors or gods, or gateways which acted as a means of communication with other worlds, or the place of creation". They go on to argue that the shape of the eastern edge of Roche Rock itself, when approached from the north or south-east, has the appearance of a stone head, which, resembles an Easter Island statue. "This petrified face residing on its own island above the edge of what may have been a damp wooded carr is unlikely to have gone

---

57. From 'Journeys to the Rocks: archaeological investigations at Tregarrick Farm, Roche' – Dick Cole & Andy M.Jones – [Cornish Archaeology Vol 41-42, 2002-3]

unnoticed by visitors to the Rock in prehistory and may well have been associated with myths and legends".

These 'faces in the rocks' can often be still perceived today, and if we notice them it is quite likely that ancient peoples, especially with their view of the natural world as a living being and/or the abode of spirits, would equally have done so. Because these ancient peoples left no written records, we do not know what names they ascribed to them, but we may perhaps infer that they were given the names of their Gods/Goddesses or even the names of their ancestors. We can see something of the same practice still at work today. Several natural rocky outcrops around the Cornish coast have been given the names of actual historical personages, usually from the 17th or 18th centuries, because of their supposed resemblances to those people. Examples include Dr. Johnson's Head and Dr. Syntax's Head from around Land's End. Nearby at Sennen, a rock stack out to sea was named the Irish Lady from its anthropomorphic shape, and the legend that a woman from an Irish ship was shipwrecked there and subsequently died. Here we can see how the shape of the rock has either given rise to an associated legend, or else the legend has become attached to the natural rock. Either way, it is a good example of how rocks can take on stories and legends from a previous age, and how the rocks themselves eventually come to be thought as being places inhabited by the spirit of the person themselves.

A similar process can be seen to have happened in other places. For example, in the west coast of Ireland, on the Bheara peninsula, there is a natural rock overlooking the sea known as the Cailleach Bheara stone. This was popularly supposed to be a petrified form of the Cailleach (the Hag or Crone of Celtic legend) herself, and even today fishermen place offerings at 'her' feet in the hope of a good sea harvest. In Cornwall, on Carn Brea hilltop fort, the petrified head of a giant can be seen at the eastern end of the earthworks [see chapter 9]. Also in Cornwall, there are many other similar legends of young women turned to stone for various misdemeanours, especially dancing on the Sabbath. The most-well known of these is the Merry Maidens stone circle near Lamorna, where the stones were considered to be the petrified maidens, and the two standing stones in the field nearby the Pipers who played at the wedding feast on the Sunday. Another standing stone, not far from Boscawen-ûn stone circle was called The Blind Fiddler in memory of a similar legend.

Some researchers have however gone further than this, suggesting that some standing stones themselves were either deliberately chosen, or deliberately shaped, by the megalithic people to resemble the human form, most notably the human head and face. The most well-known example of this is perhaps the West Kennet avenue of standing stones at Avebury, and some of the stones in the circle itself. Terence Meaden wrote about and extensively illustrated these 'simulacra' in his book *The secrets of the Avebury stones*[58], and more recently Paul Devereux has written about 'places with faces' in other cultures worldwide in his book *Sacred Geography*[59]. Both Meaden and Devereux suggest that these stones could be evidence of a 'dreamtime' era (similar to the Australian aboriginal one) in which objects were invested with mythic attributes, and the stones thought to carry a spirit form, known to the Aboriginals as *arumba arunga* ('spirit doubles').

If this is the case with the Avebury stones, then we should expect to find similar examples in other Stone Age cultures

58. 'The secrets of the Avebury stones' – Terence Meaden (Souvenir Press, 1999)
59. 'Sacred Geography' – Paul Devereux (Octopus, 2010)

elsewhere, including Cornwall. From time to time such stones have been observed and identified, and examples of 'stones with forms and faces' include Boswens menhir in West Penwith, Music Water menhir near St.Breock Downs, and Long Rock menhir on St.Marys, Isles of Scilly (suggested by archaeologist Paul Ashbee[60]). Other sites with suggestive stones include Duloe stone circle near Liskeard, where the largest and most prominent stone is said to resemble a Crone or Cailleach shape. All the 8 stones in the circle are at cardinal points of the compass, N, NE, E, SE, S, SW, W & NW and there is some suggestion that each stone may represent a specific aspect of the Wheel of the Year, or that alternate stones represent 'male' and 'female' shapes, being alternatively either straight and upright or rounded. Another site with a dramatic 'face' stone is Bosiliack Barrow on the West Penwith moors. Here, one of the stones facing inwards at the back of the barrow has been seen to have a very 'ancient' face-like appearance, looking perhaps like a face of the ancestors. The barrow would originally have been covered with a mound, so the 'ancestor stone' would have been designed to be have been 'seen' only by the dead, or to be placed there to watch over the dead. Such stones are known about from other sites elsewhere.

As well as rocks and stones that have suggestive faces, sometimes the whole body can be seen in the landscape. This is well attested in other places, such as on the Isle of Lewis, where the Callanish stone circle points to a mountain called 'The Sleeping Woman', forming the profile of a sleeping Goddess. In Cornwall, similar landscape features have been observed, including the hills of Chapel Carn Brea and Bartinney, forming the body of a sleeping Goddess (the name Bartinney may actually mean 'rump'). At St.Agnes, the

---

60. 'Ancient Scilly' – Paul Ashbee (David & Charles, 1974)

Beacon has another similar shape, when viewed from the ground above the Iron Age cliff castle of Tubby's Head. Her head is the southern cairn on the Beacon, her body its long north-south slope, and her thighs and legs its lower northern slopes. At Padstow in the Treyarnon area, and on St.Breock Downs, the Trevose headland forms another distinctive Goddess shape. And finally, on Bodmin Moor, a landscape figure has been observed, outlined by the shape of Rough Tor. This can be seen from various places, especially Davidstow Moor and King Arthur's Downs, where it is silhouetted on the horizon from King Arthur's Downs stone circles. All these anthropomorphic shapes are outlines by natural features in the land, that have become known as sacred hills and landscape features, and were very probably seen as such by the builders of the megalithic sites that are placed in relationship to them.

However, it is not only rocks and stones that have human faces and bodies that have been identified. There are also some stones that seem to have an animal shape. As we have seen [Chapter 6], prehistoric humans had a close relationship with animals: during the Palaeolithic period, animals were hunted and their representations painted on cave walls in what some researchers have suggested were trance states. Also, as we know from the study of indigenous peoples, it is probable that throughout the prehistoric period animals were still viewed as having a strong spirit presence that could interact with human society. One such 'animal rock' has been identified next to a Bronze Age barrow on Chapel Carn Brea, as if it is guarding the barrow and protecting the spirits of the dead within. Chapel Carn Brea was the most sacred hilltop in West Penwith, and all the barrows along the coast seem to be aligned to it. On the hill itself, the barrow is located with a dramatic view across to neighbouring hilltops, and from it a narrow passage runs through the rocks, that may have been perceived and walked as a journey into the Other World.

Animals were thought to have spirits that interacted with human beings, and each animal had a particular meaning. At Danebury Hill Fort in Hampshire, for example, the earliest features found on the site were what may have been Bronze Age ritual pits, some of which contained dismembered dogs. In the Celtic Iron Age, and probably before, dogs were thought of as chthonic animals, who provided a safe passage to the Other World. Also found were remains of horses and ravens. As we have seen in Chapter 6, ravens were thought of as emissaries between the world of humans and that of the gods, and horses also had an Otherworldly aspect, as evidenced in the Welsh tale of Rhiannon, and some depictions of the horse Goddess Epona. The appearance of animals in rocks and stones would not just have been seen as interesting shapes, but would have carried a whole range of symbolic and spiritual meanings.

One such rock on the island of St.Agnes on the Isles of Scilly has been named Nag's Head from its supposed resemblance to a horse's head. It has been noted by dowsers that this site, although a natural rock formation, emanates very powerful energies. On the neighbouring island of Gugh (joined to St.Agnes at low tide by a sandbar) there is another distinctively shaped rock, called Dropnose Point, which again resembles a human head and nose. From a cairn on the top of Kittern Hill, there is a strong visible (and dowsable) alignment to the Old Man of Gugh menhir and on to Dropnose Point[61]. This may originally have been a 'via sacra' or ceremonial path running across the land for people (or spirits) to travel from one sacred site to another, and on to a spirit form petrified into a rock.

---

61. See Meyn Mamvro no.47 for more details

To ancient cultures, spirits of people and animals, Gods and Goddesses, and the ancestors themselves were everywhere, and especially so in the land and the rocks and stones that lay all around them.

Chapter Nine

When Giants Strode the Land

Memories of giants are found woven into every aspect of the Cornish landscape, where their legends contain echoes of a mythic past that tells stories of the creation of the very land itself. Natural features and megalithic structures are both attributed to them, with the very landscape itself often being likened to the slumbering body of a huge dreaming entity. It is said that Cornwall has more giant legends than any other part of Britain, and John Michell has said of them[62]: "In the lore and legends of West Penwith the dominant characters are the giants; here in the far west these ancient creatures had their last refuge". He points out that when Robert Hunt collected his old Cornish tales in the late 19th century, he was puzzled by the detailed stories of giants that he heard everywhere. They were told to him in good faith, as stories from the personal experience of an earlier generation. As evidence of their truth he was shown relics of the old giants: their quoits, bowls, cradles, castles, walls, tombs and footprints. They were spoken of

---

62. 'The last giants of Cornwall' – John Michell [Meyn Mamvro, no.56]

as a species not very long extinct, and in their stories there were echoes of ancient foundation myths from a time before the coming of the Bronze Age and Iron Age peoples. "The old religion seems to have lingered among the rocks of western Cornwall and the Isles of Scilly long after the Bronze Age culture had triumphed elsewhere. And with it lingered the old giants".[63]

These old giants were thought to be capable of landscape engineering on a vast scale, and the shapes and patterns that they created in the land have geomythic significance. They created the hill forts as their castles, they threw great boulders across the land that marked out the energy lines, and they strode across the land in huge steps from hilltop to hilltop, marking the visible and invisible lines that make up the etheric web of earth alignments. Tales were told of their role in earth-moving, rock-piling, river-shaping, and land-sculpting. It is the western version of the Chinese landscaping known as *feng-sui*, the artificial shaping of the land to create harmonious energy flows.

One such legend involves earth shaping by a giant on the Dodman, a promontory of land that lies near to St.Austell Bay. Here there is a long earthwork that runs from cliff to cliff, and exactly divides off one hundred acres of ground. It was hacked out in one night by a giant using his magical powers. This fortification is a genuine prehistoric structure, and is known as the 'Thica Vosa' or the 'Hack and Cast'. This massive Iron Age earthwork, nearly 666m (721yds) long and over 6m (19½ft) high, encloses the headland, which is the highest in Cornwall. Over 2,000 years ago, this earthwork could have housed a series of dwellings, known collectively as a promontory

---

63. *ibid*

fort or cliff castle. The giant ruled this area, living within the fortified earthwork, and was a source of terror to the local inhabitants, as he would eat any of their children who might stray on to the headland! This rich fare gave him one day a dose of severe food poisoning, necessitating the calling in of the local doctor. This man seized his chance, and telling the giant that he needed to be bled as a cure, proceeded to fill a large hole in the cliff with his blood, thus bringing about the end of this tyrant, whose body the doctor then rolled over into the sea. The 'dead man' gave his name to the Dodman, The word may actually be derived from the Late Cornish word *'tubman'* meaning 'mound', but a 'Dodman' is also an English vernacular word for a land-snail. Alfred Watkins, who claimed to have re-discovered straight lines in the landscape that he called leys, thought that in the words 'dodman' and a builder's hod there was a survival of an ancient British term for a surveyor. He felt that the name came about because the snail's two horns resembled a surveyor's two surveying rods. Watkins also supported this idea with an etymology from 'doddering ' along and 'dodge' (akin, in his mind, to the series of actions a surveyor would carry out in moving his rod back and forth until it accurately lined up with another one as a backsight or foresight) and the Welsh verb 'dodi' meaning to lay or place. He thus decided that the chalk hill giant in East Sussex, the Long Man of Wilmington was an image of an ancient surveyor. All of this may be fanciful, but it does fit in quite neatly with the idea of a giant surveying the land and then building his massive dwelling there. Geomythically, this legend also has some other interesting points. The earthwork was created by 'magic' (supernatural forces); the giant was given to taking a human sacrifice (an ancient motif of appeasement for a supernatural deity that runs through many ancient cultures); while his own death was decidedly sacrificial and ritualistic.

This legend has a lot of similarities with the legend of St.Agnes and the giant Bolster. Again, there is a dark undertone of blood sacrifice in this myth, which, despite its simplicity, implies sacrificial rituals carried out in some forgotten era. The story concerns the giant Bolster, who originally had his stronghold on a hill known as Carn Bury-anacht, said to mean "the sparstone grave". The hill became the celebrated St.Agnes Beacon, where the midsummer bonfires were said to take place. The popular local name for the parish was St.Enns or Anns, which may indicate a pagan deity onto whose memory St.Agnes was grafted. St.Agnes in the story is a maiden pursued by the infatuated giant, who wants her for himself. Eventually tiring of his attentions, the saint, with duplicitious deviousness, asks him to prove his love for her by filling a hole with his blood. Unbeknown to the giant, the hole opens into a sea cave, and the giant's blood never stops flowing until he is dead. To this day, the spot which can be seen at Chapel Porth, is known as 'Wrath's Hole', the word 'wrath' deriving from the Cornish word '(g)wrah', meaning a witch, hag, or crone, perhaps a pre-Christian memory of Agnes before she was Christianised. The rocks hereabouts are heavily stained with iron oxide, giving them a vividly red appearance, thus providing physical evidence for the veracity of the tale.

Later, the word 'wrath' was anglicised into Ralph, and attributed to another giant, not far away at Portreath. Ralph dwelt in a deep sunless chasm along the cliffs called Ralph's Cupboard, and was wont to ambush passing ships, plucking sailors from them to satisfy his voracious appetite. Like the giant of the Dodman, and a giant who lived at Trevegean near Land's End, Ralph had a taste for human flesh, a motif that harks back to all those cultures who believed that the chief way to appease a malevolent deity was to offer them sacrifices. Perhaps the giants were only the folkloric memory of a time when pre-Christian deities were worshipped and feared by the people? Evidently, these giants were felt to be real, and were believed in. In 1602 Richard Carew wrote of the Trevegean giant: "Not far from the Land's End there is a little village called Trebegean, in English the town of the Giant's Grave, near whereunto and within living memory (as I have been informed) certain workmen searching for tin discovered a long square vault which contained the bones of an excessive big carcase and verified the etymology of the name".[64]

This verification of the giant legend with the physical evidence can also be found on St.Michael's Mount. Hereabouts lived the giant Cormoran and his wife Cormelian. Their names are very revealing. The first part comes from the archaic and obsolete Cornish word 'caur' meaning giant, but in each case the second part of the name is the name of a plant. Cormoran means 'blackberry giant' and Cormelian means 'clover giant'. Craig Weatherhill[65] suggests that these giants were originally nature spirits, or god/desses of nature. The two giants were forever transporting great blocks of stone across the land to build the fortress of St.Michael's Mount, using a jobbing hammer that they shared with the giant of Trencrom Hill, Trecobben, four miles to the north. The giants would fling the hammer across the land when needed, which is perhaps a memory of an energy

---

64. Quoted in 'Myths and legends of Cornwall' – Craig Weatherhill & Paul Devereux [Sigma, 1994]

65. *ibid*

line that runs between these two hilltop sites, that can still be dowsed today. One unfortunate day, Trecobben threw the hammer, but Cormelian, looking up for it, was blinded by the sun's light and was struck by the flying hammer, killing her instantly. The grieving Cormoran raised Chapel Rock, a distinctive rock made of greenstone, that stands at the beginning of the causeway to the Mount, and either laid her body beneath the rock, or, in another version of the legend, from the rock gave her body to the sea. The interesting thing about this giant legend is that during the 14th century rebuilding of St.Michael's, the intact bones of a giant skeleton (about 8ft tall) were found. There was no stone marker or coffin for the giant, but the body had been buried in the secret heart of the sacred Mount. The bones were reverently removed and first reburied in the north court, but in 1864 they were again transferred to a final resting place in the Mount's small cemetery. Myth, legend, history and geomantics all seem to combine in this account of the giants of the Mount.

One particularly interesting feature of the legend is that Cormelian would transport her megalithic pieces of rock in her apron: indeed one day when she was carrying a heavy piece of greenstone her apron strings burst. This motif of 'The Giantess' Apron' is one that is found in other places. The giant Bolster of St.Agnes Beacon had a wife, who carried large rocks in her apron, from which she made the three barrows that lie on top of the beacon. This 'Giantess' Apron' motif is always about a legendary figure who strides across the land, dropping stones out of her apron which form the hills and tors and cairns that we can now see. This may be a faint memory of a myth of an ancestral Goddess who created the land, and indeed, in some places, particularly Ireland and Wales, this giantess is called the Cailleach, who is an ancient crone Goddess of the land.

Other giants strode across the land in geomythic ways. The giant Bolster, whom we have already met, was known to have stepped between two prominent landmarks in the Cornish landscape, some six miles apart. With one foot on St.Agnes Beacon, he placed the other on the hilltop of Carn Brea, which itself has a giant legend. The petrified head of the Carn Brea giant can be seen at the eastern end of this rocky outcrop, while his hand can be seen at the opposite end of the great system of prehistoric earthworks that surround two of it summits. Carn Brea was a Neolithic and Bronze Age tor enclosure, and it is perhaps these impressive earthworks that convinced later generations that they must have been made by giants. The giants of Carn Brea are said to have buried great treasures in labyrinthine tunnels that were supposedly honeycombed into the hillside, secured by terrible and potent spells. Anyone who disturbed the treasures evoked the vengeful wrath of the giants and their elemental guardians, the fairy spriggans. The guardian spells of the giants are given in some tales as invoking floods, storms, thunder and lightning, according to the time of year when the despoliation took place. All these legends show the power of a supernatural deity, working through the landscape and able only to be mediated by a shaman able to control the weather.

Another such tor enclosure further west was Carn Gulva, near the north coast of West Penwith. Here also dwelt another giant, Holiburn, who was befriended by a local lad who used to frequently visit him. They played the game of hurling, throwing large stones around the countryside, some of which can still be seen today. There is a Bowl Rock near Trencrom Hill, thrown there presumably by the giant Trecobben. The game of hurling played by Holiburn and his young friend however ended tragically. One day the young lad won the game on his own merits, and a delighted

Holiburn patted him on the head, only to crush his skull. Holiburn later grieved himself to death.

These giants in the Cornish landscape are always associated with hills and tors, and their striding across the land (or throwing hammers or stones) made a pattern that can be dowsed today as an energy line, which are themselves perhaps a trace of the processional paths that people walked between these sacred hilltops. This leads us to the notion of 'Songlines' in the landscape, which we will explore in more detail in the next chapter. But as a bridge to that, we finish with a giant legend that seems to hint at a deeper meaning than the story appears to convey on the surface. This giant legend is entitled 'The giants of Towednack'[66], which Weatherhill & Devereux say[67] "contains elements so old that they may have descended from pure mythology".

In the story Long Tom is transporting barrels of ale by ox-drawn wagon from Marazion to St.Ives by the old road when he finds that the giant Denbras the hurler has built great stone hedges across the road. Tom disputes the giant's right to block the road and challenges him to single combat. However, when Tom sees how old and enfeebled the giant is, he takes care not to harm him, though Denbras accidently impales himself on an axle and dies. Before he expires however, he acknowledges Tom's fairness and bequeathes him his castle and entire estates. To honour the giant, Tom builds a great dolmen over his grave, which may have been an actual site in the land. Tom brings his childhood sweetheart Joan to the castle, where

---

66. 'Hearthside Stories of West Cornwall' – William Bottrell. First Series [1870]

67. 'Myths and legends of Cornwall' – Craig Weatherhill & Paul Devereux [Sigma, 1994]

they marry and raise a family. One day however a travelling tinner known as Jack the Hammer appears and disputes Tom's right to block the highway, and a fight ensues. Tom wins the wrestling in the fight, but Jack wins with his staff, and they both end up as friends. Jack moves into the castle with Tom and Joan, and discovers new reserves of tin in the area, which enriches everyone's lives. Jack becomes betrothed to Tom's eldest daughter Genevra and builds a fortified home for them on the hilltop near Morvah (Chûn Castle). Firstly he has to get rid of a troublesome giant on the hill, and when he has done this Jack and Genevra get married on the Celtic festival of Lughnasa (Aug 1st) at celebrations that are continued to this day as the Morvah Feast. The people danced around the capstone of a ruined dolmen called The Giant's Stone, which marked the grave, perhaps of Denbras, or of the Morvah giant, or even in later times, Jack himself.

So who are these characters in this rather strange story and what do they represent? The route that Tom takes from Marazion to St.Ives is likely to be the ancient trackway, now called the St.Michael Way. Its significance as an ancient right of way is shown by the fact that whenever anyone blocks it (Denbras, and then Tom himself) there is a challenge to that. This ancient route may have been used in prehistoric times to transport important commodities, perhaps tin that was mined in Cornwall and used in the manufacture of bronze, or perhaps even greenstone axes, which were highly prized in the Neolithic period and exported from Cornwall to other parts of Britain. This would make the trackway very ancient indeed, and confer upon it a free right of passage. The route goes past Trencrom Hill, from where the giant Trecobben threw the hammer that killed Cormelian. So giants, trackways and ancient sites are all linked together in this tale.

As for Jack, Brendan McMahon has suggested[68] that he may be a folk memory of a prehistoric shaman. He has a magic coat (black bull hide) that recalls Palaeolithic cave paintings of priestly figures dressed in animal skins, and also modern descriptions of North European shamans who wear the skins of animals to communicate with the divine beasts with which the community identifies. As a mark of their favour, the animal god or goddess confers magical powers on the shaman, as well as secret wisdom, and in the Cornish stories a divine bull does the same upon Jack. Jack also brings divine skills to the people, such as brewing and tilling the land, and shows Tom how to work metals, especially iron. He may thus be a folk memory of the coming of the Iron Age into Cornwall, when iron-smiths, such as Jack, roamed Europe from the Halstatt in Austria, bringing with them knowledge of the manufacture of iron.

The stories of Denbras, Tom and Jack are strongly magical in character, and take place in a world beyond the constraints of everyday life, the world of myth and legend. Weatherhill & Devereux identify Jack with the Celtic god of light Lugh and say[69] "Like the Lugh of the Irish myths, he arrives as a stranger to a chieftan's stronghold, and displays an array of talents which make him a people's champion. He even originates a Lughnasa festival". Whether he is a prehistoric shaman, or the memory of a Celtic god, Jack is evidently from a mythological past that is woven into a contemporary Cornish tale of magic, pagan activities and encounters with supernatural giants. It is perhaps a tale that was first told around Bronze or Iron Age hearths, or

---

68. 'A Cornish shaman' – Brendan McMahon [Meyn Mamvro no. 28]

69. 'Myths and legends of Cornwall' – Craig Weatherhill & Paul Devereux [Sigma, 1994]

spoken or sung as people travelled the land between the places named in the story. It is an ancestral myth, and it is to more of these ancient stories that we now turn.

Chapter Ten

Songlines: Legends in the Landscape

Songlines are a phenonema of the native Australian aborigine people, but something similar may have been present among many other indigenous peoples in other countries. In Australia a songline, also called 'dreaming track', is one of the paths across the land (or sometimes the sky) which mark the route followed by localised 'creator-beings' during the Dream-Time, or Dreaming. In their culture, the ancestors of the aborigines sang the land into existence, and sang special stories about each sacred site. These stories are linked together in 'songlines' that stretch right across Australia. The paths of the songlines are thus recorded in traditional songs, stories, dance, and painting. A knowledgeable person is able to navigate across the land by repeating the words of the song, which describe the location of landmarks, waterholes, and other natural phenomena. In some cases, the paths of the creator-beings are said to be evident from their marks, or petrosomatoglyphs, on the land, such as large depressions in the land which are said to be their footprints. By singing the songs in the appropriate sequence, indigenous people could navigate vast distances, often travelling through the deserts of Australia's interior. The continent of Australia contains an extensive system of songlines, some of which are of a few miles, whilst others traverse hundreds of miles through lands of many different indigenous peoples, peoples who may speak markedly different languages and have different cultural traditions. The rhythm is what is crucial to understanding the song. Listening to the song of the land is the same as walking on this songline and observing the land.

Aboriginal Creation myths tell of the legendary totemic being who wandered over the continent in the Dreamtime, singing out the name of everything that crossed their path - birds, animals, plants, rocks, waterholes - and so singing the world into existence. For example, The Yolngu people of Arnhem Land in the Northern Territory tell the story of Barnumbirr, a creator-being associated with the planet Venus, who came from the island of Baralku in the East, guiding the first humans to Australia, and then flew across the land from East to West, naming and creating the animals, plants, and natural features of the land. In another story, the Rainbow Serpent followed a path across Northern Australia, creating rivers and mountains as she went, and stopping at especially sacred places, such as Ubirr. A song created by her is still sung by indigenous Australians, and describes her journey, and the features along it.

Other cultures all around the world had stories of ancestral beings and the paths they took across the land as it was being formed, and they would re-tell these stories, perhaps of an evening around the communal hearth, or perhaps out in the land itself as they walked across it. As so often with oral tradition, these stories might be changed or modified over time before they eventually come to be written down in some form or another. Many archaeologists[70] and anthropologists now believe that in Britain indigenous peoples would have had similar stories to tell or sing that were associated with journeys across the land and the features and megalithic monuments built along the way. Is there a way we could recover any of these stories in Cornwall? The main sources that we have are the collections of folk tales by William Bottrell and Robert Hunt, that we have already mined for evidence of the fairy realm, animal totems and the Celtic Otherworld. But could they also give us insights into traces of possible Cornish 'songlines' from the prehistoric period – stories written about the creation of the land and of travelling supernatural routes through the landscape?

One of the best candidates for this is the tale of An' Pee Tregear[71], recounted in Chapter 4, which takes place on 'All-Hallows Eve', that is the old Celtic festival of Samhain, when the doors to the Otherworld are opened. This could be a songline-type story because it is so precise about the route Pee took home to Pendeen from Penzance, after she had placed some kind of psychotropic substance on her eyes. It says in the story that "she didn't go via Polteggan Bottom and Boswednan though it's the nearest. Instead she took her course through Castle Horneck fields". These routes can still be plotted on a map. The direct route through Boswednan is still a pathway today running parallel to the A3071 road to

---

70. See for example 'A phenomenology of landscape' – Christopher Tilley [Berg, 1994] & 'Stone worlds: narrative and reflexivity in landscape archaeology' – Barbara Bender et.al. [Left Coast Press, 2007].

71. 'Hearthside Stories of West Cornwall' – William Bottrell. Second Series [1873]

St.Just, while the path she took through Castle Horneck runs northwestwards towards Madron. Part of this is an old churchway route, used for travelling to churches, and taking coffins to be buried. Paul Devereux[72] has suggested alignments of ancient sites were really related to shamanic practices, and that this idea survives in Europe as death roads, corpse paths, and churchways. He identified one such route running from Penzance church, north-west through Madron and Lanyon Quoit[73], and this may well have been the route that Pee takes, while under the influence of the psychotropic substance. She has a number of strange experiences along the way, including mistaking a gorse bush for a horseback rider, before ending up in a bog at Boslow (Bosullow). Here, in her altered state of consciousness, she sees some piskies threshing the corn, who, once they become aware of her, vanish. These piskies are no twee Edwardian gossamer-winged creatures, but much more earthy nature spirits: indeed the principal thresher's face is described as being like "great round owl's-eyes", his body having "naked arms and legs out of all proportion", and his feet "splayed like a quilkan (frog)".

She then makes her way up to Dry Carn and thence passes quickly over the road near Carn Kenidjack and down the Gump, a place described as a "haunted track" that everyone dreaded. Bottrell says[74]: "Few go near that wisht place, about the turn of night, without hearing, if not seeing, the Old One and his hounds, hunting among

72. 'Shamanism and the mystery lines' – Paul Devereux [Quantum, 1992 & 2000]

73. See Meyn Mamvro no.24 [Summer 1994]

74. 'Hearthside Stories of West Cornwall' – William Bottrell. Second Series [1873]

the rocks for any restless spirits that may have strayed so far from the churchyard ... or some other frightful apparitions, fighting and howling round the carn, or fleeing over the downs". It seems that Pee has continued to take a 'ghost road', that is, one where the Otherworld and the spirits of the dead manifest. This may be a very ancient track indeed, one that the prehistoric people walked, telling stories of the spirit world, long before the modern roads were built.

An' Pee is now near home in Pendeen, but before she can get there, she has a vision of a "feasten market", a festival where fairies are dancing about a maypole. This is obviously a Beltane (May Day) festival, another magical time when the doorway to the Otherworld is opened. During this festival, she sees one of the little people drinking out of a poppy-shaped goblet, which reinforces the idea that all of this is taking place while under the influence of some mind-bending substance. Eventually the vision vanishes, but Pee has further troubles, when the piskies set upon her and mislead her path, until she gives up and lies down to sleep, where she is found the next day by the Squire at Pendeen. Her 'trip' (in both senses of the word) has been along an ancient spirit path in an altered state of consciousness, one that may well have been walked by prehistoric peoples following the 'songlines' of the land.

'The Fairy Master' is another story of Bottrell's.[75] Grace, a young girl, is fed up with being at home near Carn Kenidjack, with only her grandma's old gowns to wear, so she decides she will go into service. She goes

---

75. 'Hearthside Stories of West Cornwall' – William Bottrell. Second Series [1873]. I am indebted to Andy Norfolk for suggesting this story and others in this chapter.

to the Carn and there meets a "fairy Master", who asks her to come and look after his son. His name is Bob O' the Carn, or Bobby Carn, and he lives at Chypons, which is a real place and is on the map today. Nearby to it, by way of 'coincidence?' is a feature called Booby's Castle! She goes with him all the way to Chypons, and in doing so, unknown to herself, she follows a fairy path: "She didn't notice their road, and that for some time they had been walking through green lanes, hedged with trees; honeysuckles and such sweet flowers as she had never seen hung over her head". Although she is walking a real track across the land, nevertheless she is following a track into Fairyland at the same time. This is very similar to the Songlines in Australia, which exist simultaneously both in the physical world and in the Dreamtime. The path that Grace follows turns out to be one of the 'ley-lines' or alignments between sacred sites, first identified by John Michell in the 1970s.[76] This runs from Tregeseal stone circle, across the Gump (where Grace met Bobby Carn), through Boswens menhir (on a Mayday sunrise alignment), on through West Lanyon quoit, and finishing at Mulfra courtyard settlement, from where it aligns neatly on Chypons. The story mentions that they pass a grand house, which could be a prehistoric Mulfra Courtyard house, and then a place where four roads meet, and there is such a crossing of tracks on the alignment at Woonsmith. Here again we have a mythical journey through the landscape connecting ancient sacred sites. If the Courtyard House settlement was occupied at the time of the story, then it is set in the Iron Age. It is in fact a Cornish Songline: it exists on the literal

---

76. 'The Old Stones of Land's End' – John Michell [Garnstone Press, 1974]

Boscawen Un Stone Circle - West Penwith, Cornwall

The Merry Maidens - West Penwith, Cornwall

Boleigh Fogou - West Penwith, Cornwall

Balowall Barrow - West Penwith, Cornwall

Duloe Circle - Nr Looe, Cornwall

Carn Euny Fougo - West Penwith, Cornwall

Mermaid of Zennor, Bench-end - Zennor Church, Cornwall

The Blind Fiddler - West Penwith, Cornwall

Trencrom Hill - Near Hayle, Cornwall

The Logan Stone - Zennor, Cornwall

Mên Scryfa, standing stone - West Penwith, Cornwall

and the mythical planes, and the sites that stand along the way must each have had their stories, which were encapsulated in the Songline story that later evolved into the 'Fairy Master' tale, that was passed down orally for generations until written down in the 19th century.

Another possible memory of a Cornish Songline can be found in the tales of One-eyed Joan ('Joan's trip to Penzance on Christmas Eve'[77]) and Tom Trenoweth's sow ('The witch of Burian church-town'[78]). One-eyed Joan's tale seems to be a variant of An' Pee Tregear's tale, that we examined earlier: she smears some 'fairy ointment' on her eyes and, after seeing sprites and spriggans, makes her way to Penzance market, where she sees someone she knows in fairy guise stealing from a stall. By now she is "bewildered and tossicated (intoxicated)" and in this condition attempts to find her path home to Trove. She takes a road that exists today, through Tolcarn in Newlyn, and up Paul Hill to Choon, where a horse stands waiting, that takes her to Trevella. At this point it becomes obvious that this is no earthly steed, and it bolts through the air, eventually dislodging her at Clodgy Moor. Joan notes that "the devil's huntsman and his hounds" have often been seen riding this way (a Christianisation of the pagan 'wild hunt') and sure enough the devil soon arrives to claim his horse back. Most of the journey described in the story is ordinary enough, but Joan's flight on the horse seems to be a shamanic journey, part of which follows the direction of another one of John Michell's alignments: this one from St.Clement's Isle, over a lost

---

77. 'Hearthside Stories of West Cornwall' – William Bottrell. First Series [1870]

78. 'Hearthside Stories of West Cornwall' – William Bottrell. Second Series [1873]

standing stone at Halwyn, and across Clodgy Moor, on its way to Boscawen-ûn stone circle and beyond.

This alignment is also featured in the story of Tom Trenoweth's sow. Tom Trenoweth buys a sow at market, that Betty Trenoweth, his cousin, wanted to buy. She was notorious as a witch, and Tom had outwitted her before, so she had a score to settle. She was so cross at being gazumped that she cursed the sow. It kept escaping and causing trouble and got thinner and thinner, and in the end he decides to sell it again at the market in Penzance. He sets off along the main road into town and all goes well until he gets to Bojew(ans) Bottom, whereupon the sow takes off on her own across country to Leah. This section, from Bojew(ans) Bottom to Leah is part of the same alignment that goes through from Clodgy Moor to Boscawen-ûn stone circle, which was the direction taken by the horse on Joan's shamanic journey. We have already seen (Chapter 6) how sows could represent a creature of the Underworld, and were considered as guides for shamanic journeys. What we may have here in these stories, and this alignment, is a very ancient spirit line of the Otherworld that existed long before today's roads were built.

This alignment continues from Boscawen-ûn stone circle to a lost menhir stone on the west side of Chapel Carn Brea, the 'first and last' hill in Cornwall. The final part of this alignment marks yet another 'legend in the landscape'. This one is 'The Changeling of Brea Vean'[79], a story about Jenny Trayer (in Bottrell's version) or Janey Tregear (in Hunt's version) and her baby, who was

---

79. 'Hearthside Stories of West Cornwall' – William Bottrell. Second Series [1873] & 'Popular Romances of the West of England' – Robert Hunt [1871]

replaced by a fairy child and so became a changeling. Janey, who lived at Brea Vean was advised to take the child to Chapel Euny well, on the first three Wednesdays in May, and there to put it in the water three times, and to pass it round the well three times widdershins (against the sun). The route she takes from home to well and back again is over Chapel Carn Brea, on the same 'Songline' alignment at its northerly end. We therefore have at least three stories that were located in the land on the same alignment that runs from St.Clement's Isle at the south-eastern end to Chapel Carn Brea at the north-western end. Could this have been an original Cornish Songline, which was walked across the land from one site to another, a pilgrimage pathway during which ancient stories were told and sung, some of which have come through to relatively modern times? It would be quite a feat for them to have been re-told and re-told over generations of people, perhaps for thousands of years, but not impossible.

Finally, we have two stories that may contain memories of another alignment that may originally have been a Songline. These two stories are 'Duffy and the Devil'[80] and 'Nancy Trenoweth' (Bottrell)/'The Spectre Bridgroom' (Hunt)[81]. In 'Duffy and the Devil' (as part of a much longer story) the Squire of Trove goes hunting when a hare bolts out in front of him. He chases it along Lamorna Bottom to Boleigh fogou, where he goes down into the fogou to find a coven of witches dancing around a fire. The route that he takes is a mythic journey to an

---

80. *ibid*

81. 'Hearthside Stories of West Cornwall' – William Bottrell. First Series [1870] & 'Popular Romances of the West of England' – Robert Hunt [1871]

ancient site, one that starts in the everyday world and ends in the Otherworld. A similar journey through the spirit realms along the same pathway takes place in the story of Nancy Trenoweth, who is taken from Kemyel (where she is in service) on horseback by her drowned lover up the Lamorna valley and past Boleigh fogou to St.Buryan churchtown, the site of her lover's grave. This route up the Lamorna valley was undoubtedly a very ancient one, taken by those who may have landed at the safe haven of Lamorna Cove, from where a trackway led to the Lamorna plateau above, where in the Bronze Age were built the Merry Maidens stone circle and associated standing stones, and in the late Iron Age the settlement and fogou of Boleigh. The path then continued to the pre-Christian lan (circular enclosure) of St.Buryan that now surrounds the church. This ancient trackway may well have been walked for several millennia by people going from one sacred site to another and telling or singing the stories of the land.

These stories may have been about the ancestors or spirits of the dead, or the afterlife and the Otherworld, themes that have made their way into the stories collected by Bottrell and Hunt. The stories often tell of flying by means of horses, which seem to be shamanic in nature: shamans would go on out-of-body trips in altered states of consciousness, which have the sensation of flying. Such notions may even have given rise to the idea of witches flying on broomsticks. References in the stories to crows, horses and pigs, Celtic totem animals denoting the Otherworld, also seem to reinforce the idea. And the magical other-worldly nature of the stories tells us that we are no longer in the here and now, as the protagonists quickly shift from the mundane reality to the world of spirit and fairy. We may have lost the original stories and songs told and sung along these 'songlines', but enough remains for us to gain a glimpse into a prehistoric world of magic and mystery.

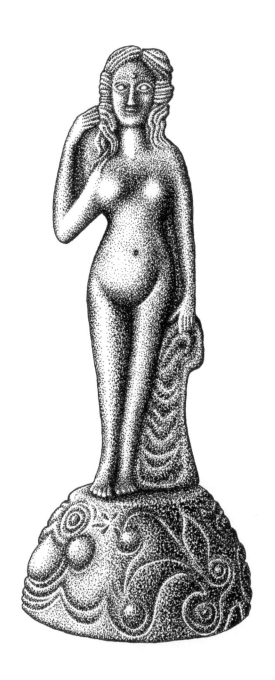

Chapter Eleven

Celtic Goddesses and Gods

I rish and Welsh legend is full of stories of the pre-Christian gods and goddesses of the land. Although these were written down much later by Christian monks, nevertheless the Celtic and pre-Celtic beliefs in the supernatural deities can be evidenced from the stories. The Irish tales were written down in the early medieval period, and the stories of the gods and goddesses are much closer to their original meaning and role in the pre-Christian society from whence they came. The Welsh tales, featured in *The Mabinogian* and *The Triads* and other tales, were written down later, and by this time the gods and goddesses, although recognisable, were often designated as kings, rulers, queens and mythological characters. We have no Cornish material this old, so evidence for belief in the gods and goddesses in Cornwall, has to be looked for in the stories, myths and legends, which were not written down until the 17th-19th centuries, by which time the gods and goddesses had all become devils, heroes, witches and spirits.

Celtic tribal society had many local gods and goddesses, and some seem to cut across local boundaries to have universal relevance. All these beings were not just abstractions, but very real personifications of the spirituality of the Celtic world, and in particular the land which was the source of their well-being and prosperity. Every river, lake and well, every wood, hill and cave had its own name and attribute, and the landscape was replete with the power of the earth gods and goddesses in their manifestation of fertility, death and rebirth. The goddesses, who were the original deities of the land, are frequently linked to a male consort who can only get his power from being married to that goddess, the sovereignty of the land. This is the true significance and meaning of the pantheon of gods and goddesses in the Celtic world, and we can now take a look at the main ones who are likely to have been worshipped in Cornwall as well as Ireland, Wales, Scotland and Gaul.

The **Cailleach** (pronounced Kaiach) was a primal, ancestral goddess, first recorded as the Cailleach Bheara from south-western Ireland, where Neolithic incomers from the Iberian Peninsula may have brought her when they came to Ireland. She was envisaged as an old, crone-like woman who could confer favours to her followers, but be a deadly enemy to those who opposed her. She may be a distant source for all the crone women who appear in the Cornish tales and legends, who are able to cast magical spells and have contact with the Otherworld, and sometimes have fairies and animals as their familiars. Another eponymous goddess was **Anu**, the original mother of the Irish gods, the mother-goddess of the land. In Ireland, the Tuatha Dé or Tuatha de Dannan were said to be descended from her (Danu = children of Anu), and her earth fertility aspect is clearly shown in the name of a twin-peaked hill in Kerry - "the paps of Anu". In Cornwall it has been suggested[82] that a strange stone head carving at St Anne's Well at Whitstone could be an effigy of Anu, spirit of the well itself.

---

82. In 'Secret Shrines' – Paul Broadhurst [Pendragon, 1988]

Some gods and goddesses were mainly tribal deities. Irish gods included the ancestor father-god **Dagda** who was linked to the land by being married to a nature-goddess **Boann** the river Boyne. Goddesses included **The Morrigan**, the triple war-goddesses, consisting of the Morrigan (phantom queen), Badhbh (crow or raven, with links to the Cornish god Bran), accompanied by Nemhain (frenzy) or by **Macha**, who again has three aspects. The first Macha was wife of a leader, the second Macha ruled over the land, and the third Macha was a supernatural bride who lived happily with her mortal husband until he violated a promise not to speak her name amongst men, a tale found in all Celtic mythologies. Each of the Machas has an association with the land and fertility through the authority of a female leader, just as the war-goddesses influence the outcome of a battle by magical shape-shifting means. All these goddesses combine features of war, maternity, youth, age and fertility, all part of a fundimental life/death/ protection symbolism. Some are represented in triple form, later called in Roman times the **Matronae**. These are often depicted carrying baskets of fruit (comucopiae), loaves, fish or children, and may be suckling their young, representing fertility and general prosperity. On some occasions they represent the fates and are linked with the Roman goddess Fortuna. One particular class of figurine that has been widely found were so-called 'Venus figurines', often cheaply made of pipe-clay material, and therefore easy to obtain by ordinary people. One such figurine was found on the island of Nor-Nour, one of the Isles of Scilly, where there was a shrine in Romano-Celtic times that was visited by sailors on their passage from Brittany to Wales and Ireland, who may have left such figurines as a thanks for, or entreaty for, a safe passage. These offerings may have been made to a local maritime deity, and it has been suggested[83] that her name may have been ***Sillina**, a Cornish/Scillies goddess who gave her name to the Isles of Scilly.

Other localised goddesses in Britain included Coventina and Sulis Minerva. **Coventina** was a goddess of sacred wells and springs, who is found mainly in the north of England. At her well at Carrawburgh in Northumberland pins were thrown into the water as an offering, a custom found at many other wells, including in Cornwall at Chapel Euny, Roche and St Michael's Mount (where the god Sol, who may originally have been a goddess, could have been worshipped). Another water goddess was **Sulis Minerva**, found at Bath, where many votive offerings, including carved ivory breasts, have been found. Sulis was originally a Celtic goddess, who was later Romanised with the addition of the Roman goddess Minerva as a suffix, and it has been suggested[84] that there was a direct link between the name Sulis in Bath, and the name Sillina on Nor-Nour, indicating that both goddesses may have been two different aspects of the same goddess of water and healing. Worship and celebration of the two goddesses may have been linked by sacred fires. Beacons were lit on holy hilltops in Cornwall in past times, and Scilly too may have had its beacon, as a flame for mariners, guiding them to the safe port of the goddess Sillina. A corresponding beacon-light may have been sited on the Cornish mainland opposite, and from here a series of bonfire lights may have run up the country to the shrine of Sulis Minerva at Bath, both sister goddesses linked in a great chain of fiery connection.

---

83. in 'Exploration of a Drowned Landscape' – Charles Thomas [Batsford, 1985]

84. *ibid*

Epona was a Celtic horse-goddess, known in Welsh legend as **Rhiannon**. Horses were revered throughout Celtic society and horses appear in many legends and stories, and have been found depicted in figurines. There is also evidence in Britain for ritual associated with horse-worship, including votive offerings of horse-skulls and teeth. The cult of Celtic horsemen seems to have been especially popular in Britain, and Epona was the primary Celtic horse-deity. She appears on many stone monuments and was probably identified both as a divine protectress of mortal horses as well as the spiritual essence of the horse itself. Irish kings were still symbolically mated with Epona as a white mare in the 11th century. In the Welsh *Mabinogian* she is associated with Rhiannon (= great or divine queen), a supernatural being who rides a white horse. In Cornwall a memory of her significance may be in the Obby Oss ceremony at Padstow where two Osses or horses dance through the streets each May Day, and formerly used to drink from a pool near the town.

Other Welsh goddesses were Cerridwen and Arianhrod. **Cerridwen** is a Welsh version of the Cailleach, a probable mother and moon goddess figure mentioned in the Welsh poem *The Book of Taliesin*, written down in the 12th century, but containing much earlier material. Cerridwen is the possessor of a magic cauldron of inspiration which links her to the cauldron of the Irish god Dagda and the Celtic god Bran. She is able to shape-shift and changes into a hound, an otter, a hawk and a hen as she pursues the boy Gwion, who is reborn as the bard Taliesin. The whole story is about the taking and giving of life, and the cauldron represents abundance and knowledge. It has been suggested that Cerridwen's cauldron is an original form of the Arthurian Grail and may also connected with the philtre from which Tristan & Iseult drink in the Cornish legend. **Arianhrod** was a Welsh goddess of the full moon and inspiration. Her name means 'silver wheel', possibly an image of the wheel of the lunar year, or alternatively a metaphor for a spider's web, which would make her a Celtic analogue of the Greek goddess Ariadne. Arianrhod dwelt on an island off the Welsh coast with her attendant priestesses, and her legend concludes with the destruction of the island and all its inhabitants, an archetypal myth present in all Celtic lands including Lyonnesse in Cornwall and Ys in Brittany.

Finally amongst the goddesses, there is **Brighid** or **Bridgit**. Found in Ireland and Scotland, she was an important maiden goddess of divination and prophecy who was later Christianised into St. Bride. She has many wells dedicated to her, including one in Cornwall at Landue near Launceston, and has given her name to rivers in Ireland, Wales and England. Her feast day was Imbolc on February 1st. and her shrine at Kildare in Ireland was guarded by 19 priestesses or nuns who kept a sacred flame burning in her honour. This idea of a sanctuary for the Goddess may have been transferred to her well at Landue, for the word 'Landue' actually means 'sanctuary'. Worship of this Goddess/Saint spread from Ireland into Wales and thence into England, where she is patron saint of Bridestowe in Devon. Her pupil St Breaca, who may be an avatar of Bridgit, came to Cornwall in the 6th century.

To turn to the Celtic gods, perhaps the principal one is **Lugh**, the hero-god of light and crafts. In the Irish tale of the Battle of Magh Tuiredh, Lugh recites his list of skills - a wheelwright, warrior, harper, hero, bard, magician, doctor, cupbearer and craftsman in metal. He is also associated with ball-play and horsemanship. His feast-day is Lughnasad, August 1st, which he created in honour of his step-mother, the goddess **Tailtu**. In some traditions it is Tailtu, whose spirit is represented in the corn, who is cut down at the harvesting;

in others it is Lugh who is the Corn King, who is cut down with the harvesting of the corn and whose spirit is re-formed into John Barleycorn. This is celebrated in Cornwall in The Crying of the Neck ceremony, and was, until the 19th century remembered at Morvah fair at the beginning of August where folktales involving a giant, a "master of skills and ingenuity" were enacted. This may well link back to an incident mentioned in the 6th century Life of St Samson, where Samson witnessed what appears to be a celebration of the feast of the god Lugh at Trigg in Cornwall, where there was "an abominable image standing on top of a hill", and a ritual enactment of the myth of the god. Lugh's name means "the shining one", and obviously makes him a sun god: in both Ireland and Cornwall his festival was celebrated on hill-tops. Irish mythology has him linked to the Goddess of the Land (the sovereignty of Ireland), Anu herself.

Another Celtic sun god is **Bel**, remembered at the festival of Beltane, meaning "the fires of Bel". In Cornwall a practically unbroken tradition up until the early years of the 20th century had bonfires lit on high hilltops and cattle driven between them for fertility and purification. There was also a custom for people to get up early on May Day (Beltane) to "watch the sun dance". Another name for Bel may simply have been Sul or Sol, meaning sun: the original name of St Michael's Mount was Din-Sol, indicating that a Celtic divinity was worshipped from the top of this sacred island. If so, it may have been an earlier sun-goddess rather than god, with her name being cognisant with Sulis.[85]

Cernunnos, known as "the stag-horned god", was illustrated on the Gundestrup cauldron, a large silver cult-bowl from Denmark, believed to date from the 2nd – 1st

---

85. See 'The Goddess on the Mount' – Kelvin Jones [Oakmagic Publications,1998]

century BCE [see chapter 6]. His image has also been found on a stone from Reims where he is associated with a stag and a bull. As we have seen, stags, boars and bulls occur throughout Irish and Welsh mythology, and were symbolic of the chase from this world to the realms of the gods. There is a strong prosperity/fertility cult association, and Cernunnos was undoubtedly lord of beasts and fecundity. On one of the plates of the Gundestrup cauldron, Cernunnos is accompanied by a snake, and this is repeated in other finds where his torc, antlers and ram-horned snake are all associated with him. Again this is a symbol of prosperity and plenty but also of the underworld. A Celtic silver coin from Petersfield, Hants, also shows him as a Celtic solar god. All these images come together in a Cirencester relief where Cernunnos, with antlers and purses filled with coins, sits grasping two ram-horned snakes which actually replace the god's legs. He may be linked to Cornwall through 'cern' in his name, which means 'horn', as it has been suggested that 'Kernow' is derived from a root form meaning "people of the horned god". There may be hint of this horned god association in the carving at the entrance of Boleigh fogou near Lamorna which appears to show a figure, carrying a stave or horn in one hand, and possibly a serpent's head in the other. As Cernunnos was later Christianised into Satan, it may also be significant that the Duffy and the Devil legend at this site [see chapter 5], involving hunting and fertility and the devil, is also associated with the fogou.

Finally, there is the legend of **Bran** and his sister **Branwen**. Their story is told in the old Welsh tale *Branwen, Daughter of Llyr*. Although not specifically named as god and goddess, there are strong hints in the story that this is what they originally were. This tale, written in the 14th century, tells the story of a Welsh king Bran (meaning 'raven') who was the ruler of 'The Island of the Mighty' (Britain). He has a sister named Branwen, which translates as White or Sacred Raven. Branwen agrees to marry Matholwch, King of Ireland, in order to secure a peace between the two nations. Unhappily the peace lasts for only a short time because word gets back to Bran that his sister is being ill-treated and abused. To avenge this insult and to rescue his sister, he gathers together a large army and crosses the sea to Ireland. He was, we are told, a giant of a man and this was to stand him in good stead, as he was able to wade across the sea carrying his harpers on his back. In that manner they kept their instruments and their strings dry. When his army comes to the River Shannon, they find that the Irish have retreated across it and have broken down all the bridges. With the words "Let him who is a chief be a bridge" Bran lays across the river and allows his army to pass over him. Then follows a bloody battle, complicated by the Irish use of a cauldron of rebirth that could revive any dead warrior. When the battle was over all the British and Irish, save a few, were slaughtered. Bran himself was mortally wounded by a poisoned dart in the foot. He gives his seven surviving companions the order to cut off his head (regarded by the Celts as the seat of the soul) and take it back with them to bury in London.

On their way the seven halt at two sacred places: Harlech, where they feast for seven years, and on the isle of Grassholm, where they feast for eighty years without noticing the passage of time, until they open a door on the side facing Cornwall, whereupon all their grief comes back to them, and they set off for a final resting place in London. They eventually bury Bran's head in a place called White Hill where it would act as a Protector and Guardian of Britain. Unfortunately, according to legend, Arthur decided that it was his job to be the Guardian of Britain and so he ordered Bran's head to be dug up and cast into the sea! This legend still carries some weight today, as the Tower of London stands on the site of White Hill and in the Tower are kept 'The Royal Ravens'.

Bran in the tale is a warrior chief of supernatural strength, who acts as a bridge, or conduit, between this world and the Otherworld. Barry Reilly[86] suggests that this would give him the status of a magician-king, and his link with the supernatural qualities of the raven would make him a very powerful deity, one well worth invoking for his divine protection. Bran seems to have been an important deity in Cornwall. There are many places named after him: Brane, Polbrean, Park-an-Vrane, Trevrane, St.Breward (from Branwalder), to name a few. This could indicate that Bran was seen as a divine protector of an area of land or settlement. Two ancient sites in particular are named after him: one is the hill fort of Caer Bran in West Penwith, which has a defensive ditch and three ring cairns in its interior that date back to the Bronze Age. Its supernatural status is enhanced by a local legend that says it is a sanctuary from evil spirits, and it is also reputed to be a haunt of the elusive small people. The other site is a standing stone called the Mên Scryfa, also in West Penwith, which means 'the inscribed stone'. It has a 5th or 6th century inscription on it that reads "Rialobrani Cvnovali Fili" which means "Rialobranus, son of Cunoualos". The first name means 'royal raven', a title which links it directly to Bran. The local legend of Rialobran tells of an unnamed enemy from the east who took the lands of West Penwith and made his base at Lescudjack Castle, overlooking Penzance. Rialobran, together with his warband met and fought this foe, but in the battle Rialobran lost his life. It is however possible that he was the victor, albeit posthumously, because the standing

---

86. 'Bran – the sleeping guardian' – Barry Reilly [Meyn Mamvro, no.78]

stone was inscribed to his memory. He was obviously a follower of the god Bran, and had probably dedicated his life to him. This Cornish link to Bran may have been recognised in the tale of *Branwen Daughter of Llyr*, where his followers carrying his head to London, open a door facing Cornwall, and all the memory of Bran comes flooding back to them.

The story of Bran illustrates for us that, although in Cornwall there are not many tales of gods and goddesses *per se*, nevertheless enough can be found in other tales and legends to show that it would have been no different to Ireland, Wales, Scotland and Brittany (Gaul) in the importance of its deities to the people, deities who could intervene in the affairs of humankind, and who needed to be honoured, invoked and called upon in the everyday world of being.

Chapter Twelve

Riding a Stem of Ragwort

"In every small Cornish village in olden times (and the race is not yet extinct) lived a charmer or 'white witch'. They were not only able to cure diseases, but they could, when offended, 'overlook' and ill-wish the offender, bringing ill luck on him, and also on his family and farm-stock. The seventh son of the seventh son, or seventh daughter of the seventh daughter, were born with this gift of charming, and made the most noted pellars; but anyone might become a witch who touched a logan (rocking) stone nine times at midnight. These logan rocks are mentioned elsewhere as being in Cornwall their favourite resorts, and to them they went, it is said, riding on ragwort stems, instead of the traditional broomsticks".[87]

Here, in this 19th century account by Margret Courtney, we have in a nutshell, the traditional attributes of the Cornish witch or wise-woman. The healing and cursing qualities of these white witches have been well documented[88], and it is not so much their spells, rites and

---

87. from 'Cornish Feasts and Folklore' – Margaret Courtney [1890]

88. See for example 'Sorcery and Witchcraft' from 'Popular Romances of the West of England' – Robert Hunt [1871], and for their survival into recent times see 'Traditional Witchcraft' – Gemma Gary [Troy Books, 2008] & 'The Black Toad' – Gemma Gary [Troy Books, 2012].

charms that we are concerned with here, as their supposed ability to 'ride between the realms'. As Gemma Gary puts it: "Witchcraft has always been practiced in Cornwall, or at least that is how it would seem. In many ways the word Witchcraft seems to be inextricably linked with Cornwall, a remote horn of land which is home to countless legends of old magic and sorcery, fantastical beings and many haunted sites which inspire the imagination to ponder the mysterious midnight goings on of Witches and the joyous gatherings of Piskies".[89] It is these "mysterious midnight goings on" that show the witches to be the inheritors of the shamans and their supernatural abilities to connect with the Otherworld.

Witches were thought to have the power over the elements. They could do something called "calling down the wind", by which means they could cause (or stop) a strong wind that could affect boats going out to sea or not. At one time, witches used to gather at Boscastle Harbour at sailing times to "sell the wind". For their money sailors received a string with three knots. Undoing the first would bring a breeze to sail by, the second would keep a gale behind the ship, and the third was best for the wind that would guide them into harbour.[90] At Chapel Idne in Sennen, it was recorded that a local "holy woman" 'brought home a west wind' to stop the Danes invading. And Madgy Figgy, "one of the most celebrated of the St.Levan and Burian witches"[91], would control the weather to bring about storms that could cause ships to be wrecked on the coast.

---

89. 'Traditional Witchcraft' – Gemma Gary [Troy Books, 2008]

90. From 'Myths and Legends of Cornwall' – Craig Weatherhill & Paul Devereux [Sigma, 1994]

91. 'Popular Romances of the West of England' – Robert Hunt [1871]

Witches are traditionally supposed to be able to ride on broomsticks, and in Cornwall there is a particular local take on that, as they ride on stems of ragwort, which of course is very prevalent in the Cornish countryside. Madgy Figgy was one such witch. She lived in a cottage not far from Rafta, but would frequent a stack of rocks on the coast called Tol-Pedn-Penwith, from where she would launch herself into the air on a stem of ragwort. This may not be as fanciful as it sounds. It has been recorded that medieval witches prepared magic 'flying ointment' from plants such as henbane, belladonna and mandrake.[92] All these contain the powerful hallucinogen hyoscyamine,

15th century woodcut showing three witches flying on a pitchfork, turning into animal forms

which gives the sensation of flying through the air. These hallucinogenic preparations were smeared on their bodies or applied with something like a feather. The ointment was thus absorbed through the skin and the hallucination of flying would follow. Broomsticks were everyday objects kept close at hand in most cottages, but if the witches were out of doors, and expected to experience the sensation of flying, a nearby stem of ragwort would serve just as well.

The riding of a broomstick or stem of ragwort has about it the notion of riding a super-natural steed, and we have already seen from Cornish stories of supernatural

92. For more details see 'Shamanism and the mystery lines' – Paul; Devereux [Quantum, 2001]

encounters [see Chapter 10] that 'flying horses' figure prominently in them. There are links here with Siberian shamans who rode horse-headed sticks through the skies of ecstatic trance to the World Tree or Cosmic Axis. Paul Devereux suggests[93] that the remnant of these traditions is doubtlessly the folk image of the hobbyhorse. He also points out that in Scandinavian mythology, Frigg, the wife of Odin, was depicted riding on a broomstick. Both Frigg and Freya were different aspects of the same Goddess, and Freya was the mistress or first teacher of seidhr, a form of trance divination. This was practised by the seidhonka, who in the course of her divination, would go into trance and have an out-of-the-body experience. Freya was said to have owned a magic feather garment that enabled her to fly. The witches flights on their stems of ragwort are therefore in a long-lasting tradition of shamanic and hallucinatory magic.

A further aspect of the shaman's flight may also have been culturally transmitted from other places. Widespread from northwest Europe to Tibet, shamans' flights are envisaged as an upward ascent by ladder to the Otherworld. Sometimes the ladder was placed symbolically against a real tree or post, and the shaman would ascend by flapping his or her arms like a bird. Sometimes notches would be cut on a post so the shaman could physically climb it. Is it perhaps relevant that where Madgy Figgy climbed to launch herself on her stem of ragwort was a 'chair-ladder'? This was a pile of cubical masses of granite piled one on top of each other, with horizontal joints representing steps up in the 'ladder'. Madgy Figgy's chair-ladder was an actual rock formation at Tol-Pedn-Penwith and can still be seen there today.

That the flying on broomsticks or ragwort was a hallucinatory experience is further evidenced by the ability

---

93. *ibid*

of the witch to change into animal form at the same time. In many trance states, turning into an animal is a very real and powerful experience. Such shape-shifting experiences have been universally recorded in many cultures and by the ingestion of many psychotropic substances. Animals experienced in this way include foxes, hares, cats and wolves (known as lycanthropy). In one medieval report, seven male and female witches confessed to rubbing ointment on their bodies, then putting on wolfskins and going on all fours and running about the country. In an experiment[94] in the 1960s, a psychologist Claudio Naranjo took the psychoactive substance harmaline, and 'became' a huge bird, a fish, and then a tiger. He said: "I walked, feeling the same freedom of movement, flexibility, grace. I moved as a tiger in the jungle, joyously, feeling the ground under my feet, feeling my power, my chest grew larger. I then experienced what a tiger feels when looking at its prey".

In some of the Cornish tales, witches turn into their familiars, especially hares and cats. In the tale of 'The witch of Treva'[95], there lived "a wonderful old lady deeply skilled in necromancy". One day her husband got into a rage because there was no food in the house, so she turned into a hare and ran all the way to St.Ives, five miles distant, and quickly returned with the food. At her funeral some years later, hares and a cat were seen leaping over and sitting on her coffin. In the tale of 'The witch of Kerrow'[96], the protagonist Sir Rose Price goes hunting a hare that always escapes from him. One day the hare is shot but not killed, but when the hunters follow it into a house, they see instead

---

94. Recounted in 'The Long Trip' – Paul Devereux [Penguin, 1997]

95. 'Popular Romances of the West of England' – Robert Hunt [1871]

96. 'Hearthside Stories of West Cornwall – William Bottrell. Third Series [1880]

of the hare, an old woman bleeding about her head and face. She is a shape-shifting witch, and is accompanied by her 'familiar' – a large black cat with "eyes like coals of fire, showing his teeth as if to spring at the intruders". In a tale [97] of the magician Pengersec, the spirit of a murdered woman turns into a hare and follows Pengersec around.

In another tale[98] a witch turns herself into a toad. An old woman called Alsey lived in Anthony, near the River Tamar, but when the landlord came for his rent, she cursed his wife and all he owned. Back at his shop, an enormous toad fell heavily from the ceiling, which the man then threw into the fire. Almost immediately, word reached him that Alsey had been severely burnt in a house fire. The dying toad in the fire is then thrown out into the garden where it dies overnight, as indeed also does Alsey. When it was examined in the morning "it was found that all injuries sustained by the toad corresponded with those received by the poor wretch". In all these stories, the animal into which the witch has turned is viewed as being devilish or evil, but this of course is only a later Christianisation of the memory of pagan practices, that involved shape-shifting and altered states of consciousness. In German tradition, toads were thought of living in the plant hemlock, a very poisonous substance that was nevertheless sacred to the Goddess Hecate, and has strong hallucinogenic properties. Some toads themselves also have substances on their skins that have hallucinogenic effects. In 1991 it was reported in Vancouver that people were picking the creatures up and licking the bufotenin off their bodies to experience

---

97. 'Hearthside Stories of West Cornwall' – William Bottrell. Second Series [1873]

98. 'Popular Romances of the West of England' – Robert Hunt [1871]

psychedelic trips. Toads play a large part in many Cornish charms[99] and their presumed power to kill or cure may be a memory of the time when witches were able to enter into the essence of the toad itself.

We began this chapter with an account of how to become a witch, so it is perhaps only fitting that we should end it with another account[100] of how to become a witch that involves the inversion of Christianity, the invoking of Celtic magic numbers and directions, and the presence of a toad. Once again it is Margaret Courtney who has the details:

"Go to the chancel of a church to sacrament, hide away the bread from the hands of a priest, at midnight carry it around the church from south to north, crossing east three times. The third time a big toad, open-mouthed, will be met, put the bread in it; as soon as swallowed he will breathe three times upon the man, and from that time he will become a witch, known by five black spots diagonally placed under the tongue".

Toads, hares, cats and other animals were not only 'familiars' for the Cornish witch or wise-woman, they were part of the altered states of consciousness reached by those who could attain visionary experiences of the Otherworld, a group of people who come from the same mould as the shamans on their psychedelic flights. The Cornish witch on her stem of ragwort has been on a long trip that leads back to the dawn of humanity.

---

99. See 'The Black Toad' – Gemma Gary [Troy Books, 2011] for more details

100. From 'Cornish Feasts and Folklore' – Margaret Courtney [1890]

Chapter Thirteen

The Arthurian Realms

Some of the most enduring legends in Cornwall are those from the realms of King Arthur, many of which feature stories of otherworldly beings and magical events. Cornwall has a special place in the Arthurian mythos. Although Arthur is associated with many places in Britain, especially Wales, it is only in Cornwall that there is the legend of his birth. Even the early Welsh Triads link him to Cornwall, often in a deeply mythological way. It was at Tintagel where he was born, the illegitimate son of Uther Pendragon (meaning "head of the serpent") and Ygerne, wife of Gorlois, Duke of Cornwall. An alternative legend has the magician Merlin snatching the baby boy from the sea at the cave below Tintagel head, called Merlin's Cave, This places Arthur in the tradition of a supernatural being, given to humankind by the Sea Goddess herself. Geoffrey of Monmouth, a Welshman writing in the 12th century, claims that Arthur was born in Cornwall, calling him 'The Boar of Cornwall'. This link of Arthur to the boar is further reinforced in a late 12th century tale, Culhwch and Olwen, in which Trwyth the boar is chased by Arthur into Cornwall, where he makes a last stand before disappearing into the sea.

As we saw in Chapter 6, boars are often represented as magical animals, and those associated with them as mythologised beings associated with the Otherworld. The name Arthur, which means 'great bear', has also been interpreted as the generic name for a tribal leader, owing his allegiance to an animal ally that was a bear.

Many of the magical Arthurian elements in the early Welsh tales point to a pagan origin of Arthur as a sun-god incarnate in a human body. There was much interchange of these traditions between one Celtic country and another, so that when the Breton jongleurs in the Middle Ages reworked the old Arthurian material into the romances we know of today, they subconsciously incorporated strands of the old pagan mythos into it, even if they did not fully understand its implications. Pagan gods and goddesses make their appearance in the Arthurian matter, suitably disguised as knights and ladies for the courtly Christian consumption of the Middle Ages.

Examples of this can be found in the stories surrounding Arthur's life. He comes into his own power when he draws the sword from the stone. The stone is Excalibur, though Geoffrey of Monmouth calls it Caliburn, from the Welsh 'caleduwich' and Irish 'caladboig', meaning 'lightning sword', which associates it with the pagan Celtic thunder-god Taranus. The drawing of the sword from the stone has hints of a classic initiation ritual, whereby potential rulers and kings had to gain their right to rule from the Earth Goddess, who would only confer that right on the person who would defend the land and all its people. This notion is reinforced by a natural feature called 'King Arthur's Footprint' on Tintagel headland. This footprint-shaped indentation in the rock may well have been a place for the inauguration of kings and rulers of this Cornish land of Dumnonia in the early medieval period. This practice is known about in other Celtic lands, such as Dunadd on the Mull of Kintyre, the isle of Islay on Eilean Mor in Loch Finnigan, South Ronaldsway on Orkney, and at Clickhimin on Shetland. In all these places, the local kings could not rule unless they gained their authority from the land, who in earlier times would have been the Goddess of Sovereignty.

Other numinous places in the Arthurian mythic landscape include St.Nectan's Glen, near Tintagel, where Arthur and his knights gathered before setting out to battle. This is a place much redolent with mystery and mystique, and legend has it that it was occupied by the early Christian saint Nectan in the 6th century (whose name may derive from a Celtic water god, Nechtan). The association of Nectan with this place was made by the Rev. Stephen Hawker in the mid 19th century, but he was only adding a mystique to a place that was already considered to be otherworldly and holy.

Arthur's legendary exploits take him all over the country, but after the battle of Camlann and the death of Arthur, his sword is taken to a lake, identified with Dozmary Pool on Bodmin Moor, and thrown into the water, when a hand emerges from the watery depths belonging to the Lady of the Lake, and takes back the sword. This may be a late memory of the power of kingship and right to rule over the land being taken from and given back to the sovereignty goddess. Finally, Arthur's body is taken to Avalon, an island paradise, perhaps a mythical place of the Otherworld, but perhaps the Isles of Scilly, lying 28 miles off Land's End. Two islets on the Scillies are named Great and Little Arthur, and Professor Charles Thomas believes[101] they may have taken over Arthurian associations as the 'islands of the dead'. Arthur's journey to Avalon is reminiscent of pre-Christian

---

101. 'Explorations of a Drowned Landscape' – Charles Thomas [Batsford, 1985]

boat burials, and links Arthur into an ancient tradition that has its roots in a Celtic and Iron Age society that lies at the dawn of Cornwall itself.

This leads us to a consideration of another named tribal leader who had a boat burial and may also have originally been a sun god. Andy Norfolk has suggested[102] that the story of Gereint, an early Cornish saint and king who gave his name to the village of Gerrans on the Roseland peninsula, contains elements that date back to a pre-Christian origin. In the legend[103] of Gereint, he is supposed to have lived at Dingerein Castle, an Iron Age hill fort, and to have been buried under Carne Beacon, a large Bronze Age burial mound, in a golden boat with silver oars, in which he was ferried across Gerrans Bay.

There are references in various historical writings to a hero or saint, who is variously called Gerontius, Geruntius, Gerennius, Gerent, Geraint, etc, who may all be variants of Gereint. The accounts and the Arthurian stories are all garbled to some extent, but there is a story in the Welsh collection of traditional tales called the Mabinogian, written down between about 1300 to 1325, entitled "Gereint, son of Erbin" that is based on the Cornish king, or a god he was named after. It includes references to Edern son of Nudd, but it is probable that Edern and Gereint are the same person, confused by the story teller. It is likely that Erbin is the son of Gereint, and Gereint is the son of Lud. Lud is the same god as Nudd, Nodens and Nuada of the Silver Hand. This makes Gereint the son of a powerful Celtic deity, god of the underworld and owner of one of the four Celtic treasures, a sword fatal at every stroke. This tradition may be the result of the royal tradition of trying to trace a lineage back to a god to help establish the "divine right" to rule.

---

102. In 'Gereint: a lost Cornish sun god' – Andy Norfolk [Meyn Mamvro, no.26]

103. 'Popular Romances of the West of England' – Robert Hunt [1871]

The legend of "Gereint, son of Erbin" in the Mabinogian is probably a late grafting of chivalric tales onto an ancient Celtic myth hidden in the stories passed down through history. The final part of the tale is about a Journey through a Celtic otherworld, involving an encounter with Death, the help of The Little King, and a challenge to the death at some Enchanted Games at the court of Earl Owein. It seems likely that Gereint, Edern (a killer of giants and bears) and Gwynn ap Nudd (lord of the underworld) are the same character, perhaps a triple god. The Little King is identified by Ward Rutherford[104] as the god Belinus. He also suggests that Uther Pendragon is Bran, whom we met in Chapter 11. Another Arthurian character in Cornwall, Gorlois (husband of Ygerne, mother of Arthur) appears to have hidden mythological significance because Gorlois' name may mean the "green man". So it appears that Bran duped and killed the vegetation god to bring about the birth of the young solar hero Arthur, representing renewed fertility in the land. In the story, Gereint descends into the underworld and carries out a ritual sacrifice to renew the land, making him a god of the underworld and a returning solar king.

The legend of the burial of Gereint in Cornwall with the golden boat and silver oars ferried across Gerrans Bay may be long-held memory associated with this legend. Andy Norfolk suggests the following interpretation: "Perhaps a king died or was ritually murdered and carried ceremonially to Carne Beacon for burial to promote the fertility of the land. But it may have more to do with Gcreint being a local variant of Cemumnos and astronomical events representing his death and rebirth. If you stood on Carne Beacon at dusk at mid-winter in the Bronze Age you would probably have seen the dying sun/fertility god set over Pednvadan Point. If you had stood on Pednvadan Point at dawn at mid-summer you would probably

---

104. 'Celtic Mythology' – Ward Rutherford [Thorsons reprint, 1995]

have seen the sun/fertility god rise renewed over Carne Beacon. No doubt when the sea was calm there would have been an impressive path of reflected light across Gerrans Bay. I think this explains the legend of the golden ship with silver oars."[105]

Another Cornish legend from the Arthurian canon is the tale of Tristan and Iseult at the court of King Mark. The story of Tristan and Iseult, written down in 1160 from much earlier sources, is a tale of pagan magic, love and betrayal. Iseult the Fair was the daughter of Iseult, Queen of Ireland, and is brought back to Cornwall as bride for King Mark by Tristan, a Celtic prince and nephew of Mark. On the way Tristan and Iseult drink a magic love potion intended for Mark and fall deeply in love. She escapes Mark's court with Tristan, but later returns to Mark when the potion fades. However, their love continues even after Tristan leaves Cornwall for Brittany, where he marries another Iseult - of the White Hands. Eventually he is mortally wounded in battle and dies, having been tricked into believing Iseult the Fair will not come to him with her healing potions. When she does arrive and learns of this she herself dies of despair. The two lovers are brought back to Cornwall and buried side by side in graves, from where a hazel and a honeysuckle plant grow forever entwined.

Iseult is a Goddess figure: a powerful and independent woman in her own right, who will not be constrained by the conventions of an arranged marriage. She is the daughter of a Queen, indicating a matrilineal descent in her background, and both Mark and Tristan's position is dependant on the power of her love. She is able to control people and events, as for example when she tricks Mark by getting Tristan, disguised as a beggar, to carry her across the Perilous Ford, and she is also a natural healer. It is therefore possible that in earlier versions of

---

105. 'Gereint: a lost Cornish sun god' – Andy Norfolk [Meyn Mamvro, no.26]

the tale she was the Goddess of the Land, to whom the King or Prince had to be wed to gain his power. The significance of Tristan marrying another Iseult when her love is no longer available to him should not be overlooked in this context. The two Iseults are two aspects - and with Queen Iseult there are three - of the same archetypal figure, the Sovereignty of the Land herself.

Iseult the Fair also has parallels with other independent and rebellious women against the constraints of patriarchal society, such as the flower-bride Blodeuwedd from the Mabinogian, Blathnait from the Irish myths, Grainne from the Irish cycle of Finn, and Gwenhwyfar (Gueinevere) from Welsh and British legend. Iseult may be a combination of a local vegetation Goddess (whose name has been lost), and also a Cornish variant of Bridget/Bride, who may have been known through long years of sea trading with Ireland. Bridget may have been brought from Ireland specifically by Irish pottery makers, who came to settle in Dumnonia in the 6th and 7th centuries. In the Welsh Triads, Tristan is also a powerful swineherd, indicating his link to the Underworld and his rivalry with Mark over the hand of Iseult places him in the ancient context of the theme of the fight of the Summer and Winter kings over the hand of the Spring maiden, a theme deeply rooted in the British and Celtic mysteries. The legend of Tristan and Iseult is full of many such echoes of a time when Iseult was not merely a "fair princess", but a powerful and central Goddess figure in her own right.

All these stories from the Arthurian canon and Cornish legend point to a mythology in which the heroes and kings, and the princesses and saints featured in them are not merely characters in stories, but carry a strong resonance of the gods and goddesses that they may once have actually been. The worlds of magic and mystery depicted in these stories are the realms of the deities themselves.

Chapter Fourteen

Saints and Serpents

There are many stories of the early Saints in Cornwall, of whom it is said that there are more of them than there are in heaven! These hagiographies are some of the earliest orally transmitted material that we have in Cornwall, and these saints' stories seem to inhabit a supernatural world that is at the same time rooted in the local landscape.

Many of the Cornish saints are found only in the Celtic lands of Ireland, Wales and Brittany, and most of these early holy men and women seem to have moved freely between these countries, mainly by sea. They existed at a period that was the interface between paganism and Christianity, and therefore many of them have strong pagan elements in their stories. Many of the stories tell of the arrival of saints in Cornwall, including St.Piran who floated over from Ireland on a millstone and arrived at Perranzabuloe, and St. Ia who floated over on a leaf to St.Ives. It has been suggested that the 'mill stone' and the 'leaf' may have in fact been coracle boats that were used during the 5th and 6th centuries to travel the seas, but equally the image may be a symbol of the almost supernatural appearance of these early Celtic Christian missionaries, appearing to arrive 'out of the sea'. St.Budoc, who gave his name to Budock Vean in Constantine, was said to have been born in a cask at sea, which makes his birth a miraculous one, perhaps birthed from the Sea Goddess herself.

When many of the saints arrived, often the first thing they did was to plunge their staff into the ground, whereupon a fresh spring of water would gush forth. St. Petroc, arriving at Little Petherick near Padstow, did this, and this legend may refer to the taking over by early Christian missionaries and hermits of the natural springs and holy wells, so beloved and resorted to by the people. Sometimes this water seemed to have magical qualities. St.Ludgvan prayed for water and was rewarded by the appearance of a crystal clear stream. The saint washed his eyes in the sparkling water and dramatically discovered that it enabled him to see microscopic objects. He then drank the water and found that he then possessed a great fluency of speech. Finally he prayed that all children baptised in the stream would escape the hangman's noose, which proved to be correct, as one Ludgvan woman who was later hanged was found to have been born and christened in a neighbouring parish!

Many of these natural wells and springs were places where the early saints built their cells and chapels. These include Sancreed, Chapel Euny, St. Levans, Chapel Jane, St.Clethers, St.Neots, St.Michaels (at Michaelstowe) and St.Ruans (on the Lizard peninsula). Many of these wells had miraculous healing powers, usually for specific ailments. For example, Chapel Farm well at St.Breward, Castle Horneck well in Madron, Nance well at Colan and Joan's Pitcher well in Lewannick were considered good for sore eyes, while St.Levans well at Porthchapel cured both eyes and toothache; St. Nuns well at Alternun cured insanity; Alsia well in St.Buryan and St.Pirans well in Perranzabuloe were good for rickets, whilst weakly children were bathed in Menacuddle well at St.Austell. Jesus well in St.Minver was reputed to cure whooping-cough; while sickness of all kinds could be cured at Chapel Euny well at Brane, Constantine's well at St.Merryn, Dupath well at Callington, Lady well at Mevagissey, and St.Madderns well at Madron. It is unlikely that people would continue to go to these places for healing over many centuries unless the cures were perceived to work. It may be that there were specific minerals in some of the waters that aided particular kinds of healing[106], but it is more likely that it was a belief in the efficacy of the cures that produced the desired effect. This 'mind over matter' syndrome is well attested in native cultures such as voodoo, where the suggestion by the 'witch doctor' or shaman about the patient's state of health can play a large part in that person's recovery or otherwise.

As well as their association with healing, some of these Celtic saints had a strong affinity with the natural world. St. Neot in particular was the Cornish equivalent of St. Francis of Assisi, and he provided sanctuary for a fox and a doe who were both being hunted. When the saint's oxen were stolen one night by thieves, wild stags came to his cell from the forest and voluntarily offered themselves for yoking at the plough. St.Ruan had an affinity with wolves, and in fact while in Brittany he was accused of being one in disguise! These stories show that the early holy men and women in Celtic Christianity were very much at one with nature, and may have taken on the role previously fulfilled by the shamans and druids who could become as one with the soul or spirit of the animal world. This in turn may even go back as far as the palaeolithic shamans, who would draw

---

106. See 'The healing properties of holy wells' – Marina Boyd [Meyn Mamvro no.21]

the animals on the walls of their caves that they hunted, and paint the interaction between the human and animalistic spirit worlds.

There is a relatively large amount of material relating to the saints and their interaction with serpents. Serpents are usually represented as troublesome, and may be symbols of the old pagan religion, but the saints do not always kill them to subdue them. In the story of St. Carantoc, he is asked by King Arthur to deal with a serpent "which annoyed the country" in Cornwall. Carantoc catches it with his stole and leads it like a dog to the court. Arthur's men would have killed it but St.Carantoc stopped them and "dismissed it alive, charging it to do no more harm".[107] St.Keyne in her story deals with them by turning them into "coils of stone", and it is said[108] that their remains can sometimes be found in quarries, where they "are termed ammonites". In another story St.Samson of Dol killed a serpent in a cave near Golant, but he was notably anti-pagan, admonishing some people at Trigg for dancing around and worshipping a standing stone!

Sometimes there is a confusion between serpents and the mythological dragon, and the words 'serpent' and 'dragon' are used interchangeably. St.Petroc had dealings with a 'dragon', but like St.Carantoc he treated it kindly. Roscarrock[109] says of him: "His charity was so great that he did not only manifest it towards his even Christians, but also on a very dragon, who being in the desert, wounded in the right eye, lingered three days about his cell without doing harm in

---

107. From 'Lives of the Saints' – Nicholas Roscarrock (1548-1634) Published 1992

108. In 'Popular Romances of the West of England' – Robert Hunt [1871]

109. 'Lives of the Saints' – Nicholas Roscarrock (1548-1634) Published 1992

hope of help, he sprinkled him with water and dust mixed together and plucking put the wooden stake which stook in his right eye, dismissed him cured". Roscarrock seems to set Christianity on one hand, and the more primal power of the dragon on the other, but interestingly he does not treat the dragon as representing evil or the devil. In another version of Petroc's life in the National Library in Paris, retold by Canon Doble in the 1930s, St.Petroc catches – and releases – a dragon. A pagan king of west Cornwall, King Teudar, collected "various serpents and noxious worms" in a marshy lake into which he threw criminals. When Teudar died, his son forbade the practice to continue, with the result that the serpents ate each other until only one was left – "a horrible monster of enormous size who tore to pieces cattle and men in fearful fashion with his savage jaws". Petroc caught this dragon-serpent with his handkerchief or girdle and led it towards the sea and released it.

It was suggested to Canon Doble by Athelstan Riley that the Padstow Obby Oss represented Petroc's dragon, and that the teazer, who dances in front of the Oss, is really St.Petroc. According to Riley, the encounter between the saint and the dragon took place on May Day, and Treator Pool outside Padstow was the original marshy home of the serpents. Dragons seem to occupy a place very much 'between the realms'. They come from the otherworld of mythology and magic, but exist very much in this world as well. A legend[110] tells of how a dragon used to steal and eat sheep and cattle around Mile Hill near Portreath. On the eve of May Day one year, when the dragon was about to claim a sheep, it was attacked by a huge, white spotted dog. The dog tore off the tip of the dragon's tail as the sun rose and the dragon fled towards the sea. Both dragon and dog

---

110. 'Ghosts of Cornwall' – Peter Underwood [Bosinney Books, 1983]

seem to occupy a supernatural world, perhaps the Celtic 'annwn' or Otherworld, and the time of the encounter at sunrise, like sunset and twilight, was always considered to be a magical time between the worlds, particularly on this day, which was the eve of the Celtic festival of Beltane. Perhaps this story is a memory of a Beltane celebration, in which the dragon represents the winter (or god of the waning year), and the white dog represents summer, or perhaps the Spring Goddess.[111]

Dragons have been considered to represent paganism in these old tales, while dragon-slayers like St.Michael represent the take-over by Christianity. If that is the case, then perhaps that take-over in Cornwall was more harmonious and less conflict-bound than in other places, as the stereotype of the dragon slayer does not seem to easily fit the Cornish stories. The depictions of the saints killing dragons has also been interpreted as the early Christian saints using and manipulating the natural energies of the land; if this is true, then perhaps the Cornish stories are about the beneficial understanding and use of earth energies by these early holy men and women. In the pre-Christian period, local deities were thought to dwell in the trees and woods, the caves and rocks, the springs and the wells. The earth was felt to be alive, and spirits could be found everywhere, and the holy men of the tribe, whom we can perhaps term 'druids' mediated between this world and that otherworld. It may well be that the early saints became the inheritors of that tradition, and therefore needed to work with those pagan energies and spirits instead of opposing them. Perhaps these tales of the saints tell of their encounters with the supernatural forces that were thought to control and govern the universe, and

---

111. This interpretation was first suggested by Andy Norfolk in 'Cornish Dragon Lore' [Meyn Mamvro no.34]

it is these encounters with the otherworld that have come through in the remaining tales. If so, the saints were but the most recent example of a long tradition stretching back to the druids and before them the shamans, all mediators between this world and the Otherworld.

Chapter Fifteen

Other Realms, Other Realties

I n this final chapter, we examine what other traces can be found of otherworlds and supernatural beings in the fragments of Cornish rhymes, stories, myths and legends. One such story tells of Roche Rock, a rocky outcrop standing some 20 metres (66 ft) high, north of St.Austell. On the top of this outcrop is dramatically perched the ruins of a chapel, dedicated to St.Michael. In the Tristan and Iseult legend the lovers go there to visit the hermit Ogrin, who dwelt in the chapel on the rock. There was an archaeological excavation some years ago at a nearby farm, which uncovered some pits with deposits, and it has been suggested that these were the result of ritualised activity associated with seasonal gatherings close to Roche Rock [see Chapter 8]. The authors of the report of the excavation[112] suggest that Roche Rock was venerated by the people as the dwelling place of the spirits or gods/goddesses who dwelt within the Rock, and believe that the people are likely to

---

112. 'Journeys to the Rock: archaeological investigations at Tregarrick Farm, Roche' – Dick Cole & Andy M.Jones [in Cornish Archaeology Vol 41-2 (2002-3)]

have regarded the landscape as being the creation of such spirits, gods or ancestors. They suggest that stories, myths and legends would have grown up around such landscape features, and that places like Roche Rock may have been gateways for communication with other worlds. "Places such as Roche Rock were perceived as powerful liminal points, where spirits or beings from other worlds could affect the lives and well-being of the community".

The site has evidently a long history of sanctity attached to it, from the Neolithic right down to the Christian era, and one particular legend has a resonance of that sanctity. This legend tells of how one dweller of the chapel on the rock was a leper, who had a daughter called Gundred, who has given her name to a holy well that lies about a mile to the north of the Rock in a chasm in a deep wooded glade. Gundred fetched food and water from the well to take to her leper father on the Rock. This legend seems to make a deliberate link between the depths of the earth and the heights of the Rock. Gundred may thus be seen as an aspect of the Earth Goddess dwelling in the dank elemental place of the earth, but travelling from the underworld to the high upper world of Roche Rock. His realm was the world of masculine energies, with its St.Michael chapel dedication; hers the world of the inner female watery realms of the source of life.

Many high places, which may have originally been sacred to pagans, later under Christianity became dedicated to St.Michael. As we have seen in earlier chapters, tor enclosures which surround high cairns on the moors in Cornwall, dating originally from the Neolithic period, such as Rough Tor and Brown Willy on Bodmin Moor, Helman Tor, Carn Brea, and in West Penwith Carn Gulva and Carn Kenidjack, were thought of as the dwelling places of the gods and goddesses and the ancestors. These places became

Roche Rock [by J.T.Blight 1835-1911]

sacred in the minds of the later Bronze Age and Iron Age peoples, and when Christianity arrived on these shores they were re-dedicated to the saint Michael. Perhaps Cornwall's most famous St.Michael site is St.Michael's Mount, an island at high tide that lies off the coast at Marazion in west Cornwall. As we have seen in chapter 11 its original name was 'Din-Sol', indicating that it was dedicated to a sun god or goddess. It is claimed that St.Michael appeared to local fishermen on the Mount in the fifth century, and it has strong links with another religious foundation Mont Saint- Michel in France, which has the same tidal island characteristics and the same conical shape. Historically, St.Michael's Mount was given to the Benedictines, the religious order of Mont Saint-Michel in Normandy by Edward the Confessor in the

11th century. Even today it continues to attract seekers and pilgrims, and it is the one place in the world where the four great energy lines, identified by dowser Hamish Miller as the Michael and Mary and Apollo and Athena lines, all meet and cross. These lines criss-cross Britain (and Europe), and link together places of great sanctity and spiritual significance. People have always been drawn to such places, and many of them can trace a continuity from the present to long ago in the past. There are so many such places in Cornwall alone, that it would take several more books to tell the stories of all of them!

But here in this book we have been focusing on those places and people, and those stories and legends, that tell of encounters between this world and the Otherworld. As we have seen throughout this book, the traces of these are often hidden in the old legends, stories, and myths. So to finish with, let us take a look at a seemingly innocuous Cornish rhyme that may have a deeper significance not immediately apparent:

> *"See saw, Margery Draw,*
> *Sold her bed and lay on straw;*
> *Sold her bed and lay upon hay,*
> *And pisky came and carried her away".*[113]

So who was Margery Daw and what can this seemingly-nonsensical rhyme mean?[114] There is a well on Carn Marth near Lanner that is known as Margery Daw's or Figgy Dowdy's well. Other Cornish folk tales refer, as we have seen

---

113. Recounted in 'Cornish Feasts and Folk-lore – M.A.Courtney [1880] & 'Popular Romances of the West of England' – Robert Hunt [1871]
114. Many of these ideas were first suggested in 'Bride's bed revisited' – Andy Norfolk ['Meyn Mamvro', no.27]

in Chapter 12, to Madge Figgy or 'the dowdy'. All these may in fact be the same person who is really a Cornish harvest and fertility Goddess, closely related to, or identical with Bride, otherwise known as Brighid or Bridgit [see Chapter 11]. Brighid was a Celtic Goddess responsible for the fertility of the land. In Scotland she was represented by a sheaf of corn on her festival of Imbolc (February 1st), and was carried from house to house before finally being placed in a bed made of straw or hay overnight.[115] The production of food, the fertility of the land and the fecundity of Mother Nature were all key functions of Bridget, and they underlie the traditions associated with her day. The figure fashioned from corn was decorated with the ribbons, shells, spring flowers and stones, all gifts of the earth and sea. Her spirit was in the figure and she was addressed and invoked as a real 'being'.

Figures representing a vegetation spirit or corn mother were traditionally thrown into water in spring in many places to ensure the fertility of the land, and this custom appears to have its Cornish counterpart. It is recorded that children took their dolls to be baptised at Figgy Dowdy's well on Good Friday. (Dolls were also taken to Fenton Bebibell well for the same purpose on the same date. The name 'Fenton Bebibell' means 'well of the little people'.) Although this date is not Imbolc, nevertheless the custom may have been transferred to the nearest Christian date once the significance of Imbolc or Candlemass diminished. There may also be a connection between the Good Friday custom and fertility rites, because in Cornwall Good Friday is traditionally the best day to sow seeds: it was thought that on this day they would all grow. Originally Easter was the

---

115. See 'The Earth Goddess' – Cheryl Straffon [Blandford, 1997] for more details.

same time as the Spring Equinox, which was traditionally celebrated on March 25th, now known as Lady Day. This was regarded as the start of the year in medieval times, and there are many other traditions of festivals at wells and on hills linking Easter with the fertility of the land and rebirth of a vegetation deity.

Corn dollies were also involved in fertility rituals at other times of the year. In some places they were called May Dolls or May Babies, and carried from house to house on May Day. A Mother Earth corn figure, which could be four feet high, was part of the harvest tradition, but was also carried around the fields to awaken the newly sown seed. One version of the Margery Daw rhyme ends with "She sold her straw and lay in smut, Wasn't she a dirty slut", which may be a memory of the custom of taking the corn mother from her bed of straw and ploughing her out into the field, to help ensure the fertility of the land. The tradition of baptising dolls in the wells on Carn Marth and Fenton Bebibell may therefore be a remnant of a fertility ritual, possibly originally at the Spring Equinox, to ensure that the harvest Goddess made the crops grow well. The Corn Mother was probably ploughed into the fields, or grain from it was scattered into them after being blessed at the well.

Finally, the names Margery Daw, Madge Figgy and Figgy Dowdy may be derived from ancient Cornish names for this Goddess. Andy Norfolk points out that "medge" means to reap or mow; "medgeri" means a reaper; "da" means good; "dew(es)" means god/dess; and "filh" means scythe. So Margery Daw may be either "The Good Reaper" or "The Reaper God(dess)". Madge Figgy could be "The Harvest Scythe", and Figgy Dowdy "The Good God(dess) of the Scythe". In a simple children's nursery rhyme lies a world where people were deeply connected to the gods and goddesses of the season's round, and where it was part of their everyday life to honour them and perform ceremony and ritual for them. All around us in Cornwall are the traces of when the people of this land did truly live "between the realms".

Index

List of Illustrations